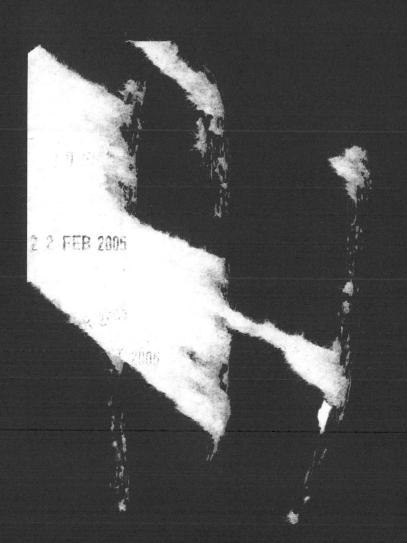

NEW LANDSCAPE DESIGN

ROBERT HOLDEN

Laurence King Publishing

contents

At the beginning of the twenty-first century the profession of landscape architecture is still really finding its way. These pages present a survey of landscape design from the past few years of the twentieth century and the beginning of the twenty-first. By nature this review is selective, and it covers projects that are significant and interesting, but in no way does it aim to be comprehensive. The book has been organized around major stylistic themes that are sometimes purely descriptive of visual form (Pattern as Placemaker; figure 1), sometimes relate to art criticism (Minimalism) or are more to do with ideas (Places of Allegory and Meaning), while at other times themes relate to a particular form of land re-use (Post-Industrial) or with the interpretation of a science (Ecological Diversity). Of course some of the projects might fit into more than one category, but they have been grouped according to qualities that are most significant from the point of view of a landscape designer. The categorization of these projects is as much to do with serendipity as it is with definitive classification. Such an arrangement allows comparison, but most significantly these categories suggest the directions in which the profession of landscape architecture - and landscape designers in general - may be heading.

Most of these projects, but by no means all, are by self-professed landscape architects. Narrow professional turf wars are irrelevant. Nella Golanda, creator of the Dionyssos Quarry development (pages 92–97) describes herself as a landscape sculptor. Battle McCarthy, who undertook the external works (i.e. landscape design) of the University of Nottingham Jubilee Campus (pages 166–171) are engineers, although they are engineers who employ landscape architects. Kengo Kuma is an architect, and the Nasu History Museum (pages 60–63) is architecture, but it is the appreciation of landscape that makes it of interest in this collection. Much of the work here is collaborative: most large landscape and urban design projects involve multi-disciplinary teams, and singling out one designer can be thought of as invidious. The work of Dan Kiley at Agnes Katz Plaza in Pittsburgh (pages 30–31) has as its *raison d'être* the creation of a setting for a sculpture by Louise Bourgeois. What is important about an individual designer is his or her direction and ability to achieve coherence. Many people may work on a project, but unless

there is a perceivable intellectual framework then it is unlikely to be of interest. It is noteworthy how many good design practices are headed by those who are academics as well as practitioners: Peter Walker was Chairman of Landscape Architecture at Berkeley until 1999; Christophe Girot is Professor at ETH Zurich; Martha Schwartz is Adjunct Professor at Harvard; Peter Latz is Professor at the Technical University of Munich-Weihenstephan; George Hargreaves is Chair of the Landscape Architecture Department at Harvard; Eelco Hooftman and Bridget Baines of Gross Max teach at Edinburgh College of Art; and there are schemes in this book by two lecturers of the University of Western Australia in Perth: Grant Revell and Richard Weller of Room 4.1.3. This list tends to prove the rule that there can only be progress through dialectic and it might suggest that an argument could be mounted against John Dixon-Hunt's opinion that: 'The subject of landscape architecture has no clear intellectual tradition of its own, either as a history, a theory, or even a practice.' Perhaps this collection of projects is fodder for such discussions.

There is also a more concrete point to be made here. This book has kept away from the forms of corporate design that are the norm in Anglo-Saxon countries. British landscape architects work in offices; French landscape architects work in *ateliers*. Landscape architecture is an economically marginal area with comparatively small budgets, yet despite this there is an alarming tendency, certainly in some countries, to view the area as a profession first - in a narrow, exclusive and limiting sense - rather than as a uniquely liberating and all-embracing activity, part art form, part scientific, part totally practical and part political.

Most of the projects included here date from after 1995, but this is not an absolute rule. Landscape design is a long-term process comparable to forestry. It is quite usual for years to pass before anything is built or planted. It is not unknown to work on a site for a decade or so and then for the site (with planning permission achieved) to pass to another owner who then changes the design team. The author has worked on designs for projects for periods of up to ten years without a tree being planted or a hole being dug. And sometimes projects are such that they involve a lifelong commitment to site. Dr Bernhard Korte's work has included a long-term commitment to Insel Hombroich since 1985 (pages 130–137).

introduction

The resulting landscape is part of a *Gesamtkunstwerk* – a total work of art – which represents an attitude to life that is promoted by the patron. Only with the patronage of an individual on an almost eighteenth-century scale can such an achievement be realized. Here, the process (not the product) of landscape design approaches garden-making, a process that can develop, change and mature. City and public patronage can also be long-term, but with so many changing political interests to represent politically this public patronage can be a double-edged sword. The long, politically complex development of the Rådhusplads in Copenhagen – which lasted from the competition in 1979 to its completion in 1995 – was just such a case (pages 56-59). The Rådhusplads is an example of a project that has been subject to political pressure. Another Danish scheme, Ørestad (pages 44-45), has been controversial from its inception when, at architectural competition stage, it was boycotted by the Danish professional architectural body. Ørestad is very much about free-enterprise land development without traditional planning controls, but in a way which much of the private sector (as developers) might well not favour. How to achieve coherent design in such a climate is something that Ørestad's designer, Jeppe Aagaard Andersen, is grappling with. Landscape design can be a long, arduous haul.

This is not a book about garden design, but the work of one avowed garden designer is included. Fernando Caruncho's work at Mas de los Voltes (pages 14-17) is a design of mown paths, wheat fields, and two species of tree. It is a late twentieth-century example of the old concept of the *ferme ornée*: indeed it recalls the plates of garden plans in Stephen Switzer's *Ichnographia Rustica* of 1718. Mas de los Voltes is more a demonstration farm than a garden, and as such it should be of interest and inspiration to all designers. Generally there is remarkably little work in these pages which can be thought of as garden-like or gardenesque – there is a lack of herbaceous plant composition in the chosen schemes. In some cases, as in that of Shodo Suzuki, it is because of a lack of faith in garden maintenance rather than through any dislike of planting. As Suzuki has written, 'Gardens represent the embodiment and symbol of landscape in man's mental image.'[2] Therefore, this lack of the horticultural and the herbaceous is not necessarily representational of the

Top: figure 1 – Carrascoplein is a scheme by West 8 which uses the land beneath the tracks of Amsterdam's Sloterdijk railway station. An example of simple pattern-making, the design incorporates white dots painted on asphalt.

Above: figure 2– The tradition of *heemparks* – a kind of nature park – has been established in The Netherlands since the 1920s. The example illustrated here is De Braak Heempark in Amstelveen.

Top left: figure 3 – The late Derek Jarman's shingle garden at Dungeness, Kent, England, is an example of artistically inspired garden-making. Jarman – an artist, film-maker, gardener and diarist – used plants with a horticultural bravura.

Top right: figure 4 – The Centre for Alternative Technology has been developed incrementally since the 1970s on the site of an old slate quarry in the Corris valley, near Machynlleth, Wales.

Above: figure 5 – Hafeninsel Bürgerpark, Saarbrücken, by Latz + Partner. Begun in 1979 and set on a former quayside area, this is the earliest large-scale post-industrial scheme. It re-uses the materials of the site and allows the natural regeneration of plants.

general direction of either landscape architecture or indeed the author's own interests. Dan Kiley, whose pocket-sized Agnes Katz Plaza is included (pages 30-31), is typical of those landscape architects who come from a garden design background. Landscape gardening, and amenity horticulture in particular - as represented by the clever horticulture of the Dutch *heempark* movement (figure 2) or the likes of the late film-maker Derek Jarman's garden (figure 3) - should not be seen as being rejected in these pages. To quote John Dixon-Hunt again, 'Gardens focus the art of place-making or landscape architecture in the way that poetry can focus the art of writing.'[3]

However, it is a useful corrective to illustrate those areas of landscape design that are insufficiently well known. The professions of landscape architecture and landscape design are not particularly high-profile. This book aims to help raise that profile.

Landscape design also encompasses the much larger-scale task of designing new urban districts or towns as Adriaan Geuze of West 8 has done at Borneo Sporenburg in Amsterdam (pages 52-55) and Jeppe Aagaard Andersen at Ørestad. Both use a landscape sensibility to model urban development, to set the rules of the game and the elements of planning structure in a way that can then allow architects to operate within that wider framework.

There is a great deal of urban design here, and whether it is an architect who is the prime mover - for example Helmut Jahn at Potsdamerplatz (pages 22-25) or Daniel Libeskind at the Jewish Museum (pages 114-117), both in Berlin - does not matter. They have worked with landscape architects in a way which allows them a stage on which to operate.

The difference between much of landscape design and architecture is that landscape design is much more concerned with process, growth, change and time as opposed to finite form, line and unchanging spaces, which are so much the concern of architecture. Therefore the inclusion of sculptural and architectonic landscape designs - such as Martha Schwartz's work at the Kitigata public housing (pages 26-29) or Batlle i Roig's Tramvia Park near Barcelona (pages 48-51) or Room 4.1.3's Garden of Australian Dreams in Canberra (pages 142-147) - demonstrate that

some projects have something more akin to stage set design or pop concert production than the usual work of landscape architects. These schemes are about place-making and the creation of a setting with a readable message, whether it is for learning about a nation's identity, as in the Canberra scheme, about finding a place to play, as at Kitigata, or for connecting communities, as at Tramvia Park. Indeed at Kitigata Martha Schwartz has needed to impose a strong coherent identity precisely because the apartment buildings were designed by architects who had been instructed not to visit the site or to work together (thanks to masterplanner Arata Isozaki's unorthodox brief). Knowledge of site is the essence of landscape architecture - there is such a thing as *genius loci*.

There is one scheme which is a subtle exception to the rule that this book is about landscape projects that have been built and planted. Northam Community Project in Western Australia (pages 138-141) is about the rediscovery of identity for a dispossessed Aboriginal community and very much about social process rather than design. The design work illustrated is therefore not as important as the process of trying to help a community re-find its place in Western Australia. It was also a process whereby students of European descent (*whitefellas*) from the University of Western Australia can begin to come to terms with what their ancestors have done to Australia's first inhabitants.

Ecological process is a significant development in landscape architecture, and one which the profession has been exploring since the early 1970s. The majority of ecological schemes illustrated here are didactic. For example at the Portland Water Pollution Control Laboratory (pages 182-185) Murase Associates have reinterpreted that nineteenth-century phenomenon, the waterworks garden, as an ecological example of publicly accessible sustainable stormwater management for the Portland Bureau of Environmental Services. Herbert Dreiseitl, of Atelier Dreiseitl, has been investigating water management throughout his career as a landscape architect, and his work is exemplary in the way it has realized processes that reverse the past one hundred years of stormwater engineering and increase natural habitat types in urban areas. The two Dreiseitl schemes featured in this book include one for Hattersheim, a small town in western

Above: figure 6 – Latz + Partner's Duisburg Nord Landscape Park, opened in 1994, is the best known example of post-industrial landscape design. A major city park was created on the site of the disused A.G. Thyssen steelworks.

Germany (pages 18-21), and one in the German capital, Berlin (pages 150-153). Both use recirculated surface water safely, in a way that also improves the environment and gives pleasure. Atelier Dreiseitl practise what so many others have theorized about. To introduce such large bodies of surface water-fed lakes into the centre of Berlin is a tribute to the firm's technical competence. Too often landscape architects resort to dead, chlorinated water, too often politicians are afraid of the elements of life.

At the Solar Living Center in northern California (pages 176-81) the educational role is paramount: it is a place to learn about the solar and water-management aspects of sustainable development - especially valuable in a country that consumes so much of the world's finite resources. The designers, Stephanie Kotin and Christopher Tebbut of Land and Place, have cultivated what was once a dump. Interestingly, Land and Place are also a design build company, so they construct as well as plant. The scheme exhibits good design build practice and is also a model of corporate patronage by John Shaeffer of Real Goods.

The following two ecological projects are on an entirely larger scale. Both the Earth Centre (pages 162-165) and the Eden Project (pages 154-157) are British projects funded largely by the National Lottery and both have spent tens of millions of pounds and done a great deal of work at first stage. They have had different histories: the Eden Project is a remarkable success with the public and is Cornwall's largest tourist attraction. The project presents different plant habitat types - humid tropical, Mediterranean, or Atlantic oak woodland - both in the open and under artificial environments. The ecology referred to here is that of habitat types, even though the habitats are totally artificial. Much of the public success of this project must be due to the promoter Tim Smit who has made full use of his previous experience as a record producer. The Botanic Garden of Barcelona (pages 172-175), by Bet Figueras, is a comparable scheme, but is being formed incrementally as a series of stages. It is, furthermore, a very good example of a strong coherent design. One suspects that in the long run it is the incremental schemes that will be more successful. 'Big bang' schemes, such as the Eden Project and the Earth Centre, need time to mature - a balanced judgement of their success should not be made until they have grown for ten

years or more. These might be compared with the Centre for Alternative Technology in Machynlleth, Wales, which has developed slowly and steadily over three decades from very small beginnings (figure 4).

The biggest shift in landscape architecture in the late twentieth century has been aesthetic. The interest in industrial archaeology, which has grown since the 1960s, has led to an appreciation of industrial heritage. Schemes from the 1980s and 1990s such as Hafeninsel Bürgerpark in Saarbrücken (figure 5) and the Duisburg Nord Landscape Park (figure 6) have led to a growth of schemes which seek to appreciate what was previously thought of as ugly. In England the National Trust's work at the former atomic weapons research site at Orford Ness is in a similar vein (figure 7). This type of work is about allowing the development of ruderal vegetation and the natural processes of disintegration while valuing industrial manufacturing processes and machinery for what they are: giant products of human endeavour. One cannot call such schemes beautiful, but they are certainly sublime. This book includes a recent project by Latz + Partner at Völklingen in the Saarland (pages 82-83) as well as Büro Kiefer's Ferropolis - an extraordinary and theatrical assembly of opencast mining machinery in Saxony-Anhalt (pages 84-87). Shlomo Aronson's project in Israel's Negev Desert (pages 98-101) follows an older tradition of ameliorating mineral extraction works. Predecessors date back to Sir Geoffrey Jellicoe's work for the Hope Cement Works in Derbyshire, England in the 1940s. But at the Negev Phosphate Works Aronson has also created landforms that are examples of environmental land art.

While this is an international survey, readers will note that Asia is underrepresented and Africa not at all. Landscape architecture began as a profession in North America. Frederick Law Olmsted is usually cited as the first to call himself a landscape architect. Perhaps because of this western origin there is an American, European and, to some extent, Japanese bias in this selection. In terms of the development of the landscape profession the situation in Asia outside of Japan is developing. Schools have now been established in South East Asia and China, and one looks forward to the maturing of these national professions. The situation in the Indian subcontinent is less developed.

However, Africa is the place of real concern. It is a continent of fragile habitats under threat, and as such needs good environmental policies. The nations of Africa need a whole range of environmental professions and expertise and they need governments who will support this growth. Landscape architecture is about much more than the cosmetic, or the creation of a showplace. In this part of the world the profession is needed for its role in landscape planning and environmental assessment, and for ensuring on the large scale that environmental damage due to development is avoided or minimized. Though the projects themselves may not always be directly applicable to Africa, the ways of thinking illustrated in this book may well be vital to that continent and indeed to the whole of the developing world.

This book follows a similar survey published in 1996 under the title *International Landscape Design*. For the author, the choice of British projects has been very encouraging compared with the dearth of them in 1996. Elsewhere some schemes have escaped inclusion because they were simply not sufficiently advanced at the time of going to press. Kathryn Gustafson's Westergasfabriek in Amsterdam promises to be a major new city park and well worth a visit (figure 8). The conservation of parts of the Bagnoli Italsider steel works in Naples, which closed in 1993 - in part a major new public park and in part a science park - is a scheme that is full of promise (figure 9).

Endnotes

1 Dixon-Hunt, John: *Greater Perfections: The Practice of Garden Theory* (Philadelphia, University of Pennsylvania Press, 2000), p.6

2 Anon: 'Shodo Suzuki: The Symbolic Cosmos', *Land Forum*, no.1, May/June 1999, pp.37

3 Hunt: *op. cit.*, p.11

4 Hunt: *op. cit.*, p.8

5 Hunt: *op. cit.*, p.9

6 Stephen Switzer: *Ichnographia Rustica* (London, J. & J. Fox et al: 1742, vol.1, p.XVI)

The intention of this book is to provide a stimulus: to collect exemplars of good design practice, to illustrate them generously and thereby provide an inspiration for students of landscape design of whatever age, experience and interest. Landscape architecture at the end of the twentieth century has become an extremely creative form of design. One may well agree with John Dixon-Hunt when he argues that, 'Landscape architecture is a fundamental mode of human expression and experience,'[4] and that '...only dance and body painting otherwise come to mind as arts that actively involve a living, organic, and changing component.'[5] In short: landscape architecture can be fun.

One common element that unites all the schemes in this book is that they fulfil Lancelot 'Capability' Brown's dictum that good landscape design is about placemaking. In conclusion, one may argue that the best landscape architecture meets the prescription that Switzer gave:

Utile qui dulci miscens, ingentia Rura,
Simplex Munditiis ornat, punctum hic tulit omne.

(He that the beautiful and useful blends,
Simplicity with greatness, gains all ends)
(after Horace)[6]

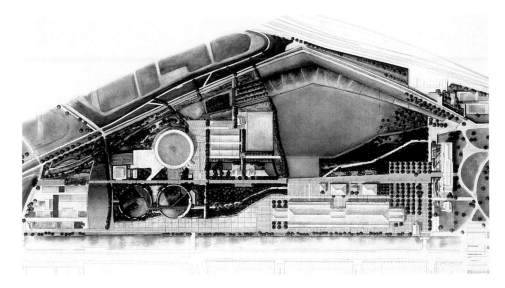

Top: figure 7 – Orford Ness in Suffolk, England, is a former Atomic Weapons Research Establishment. The site's original buildings were preserved, including the two 'Pagodas' (far left), which were used as test labs.

Centre: figure 8 – Plan of the Westergasfabriek city park in Amsterdam, by Kathryn Gustafson.

Above: figure 9 – Aerial view of the Bagnoli Italsider steelworks redevelopment project in Naples.

chapter 1 pattern as placemaker

'Pattern', used here to mean 'decorative or artistic design',[1] has been at the basis of much landscape design since Roman times - parterres of square grids can be seen in the remains of Roman gardens ranging from Fishbourne in England to the Villa of Pansa in Pompeii. 'Placemaking', on the other hand, is an eighteenth-century term used by Lancelot Brown.[2] Pattern as a basis for making places has been a constant theme throughout much twentieth-century landscape architecture, and the master of this approach is Dan Kiley. Whether working at La Défense in Paris or in the Mall in Washington, DC, he has used a regular square grid pattern to define space. Agnes Katz Plaza (pages 30-31) in Pittsburgh is one of Kiley's late works (he was born in 1912) but it shows him still applying his masterly command of grid and square in conjunction with an equally masterly Louise Bourgeois (born in 1911).

Peter Walker is from a younger, post-war generation and at the Sony Complex in Berlin (pages 22-25) he has shown once more his command of commercial pressures and constraints in his work with Helmut Jahn to create a convincing urban space. In this project Walker has used his characteristic decorative features: lines of stainless steel and light, and regular geometrical patterns of circles. Walker has been noteworthy for his pattern forming though he prefers to describe himself as a minimalist and writes, 'The result (of my work) is what I consider minimalism in the landscape.'[3] However, what singles him out as the landscape architect at the Sony Complex is his strong use of pattern as a placemaker.

A former pupil and partner of Walker, Martha Schwartz has moved towards something much hotter. She uses strong colours and themes, in a way that is often perceived as provocative - her 1999 proposal to have steel palm trees outside Marks and Spencer's store in Manchester's Exchange Square upset some Mancunians. Landscape and urban design are seen - especially in Anglo-Saxon countries - as something that should be familiar, something that becomes embarrassing when it embraces strong colours, forms or ideas. At Kitigata in Japan (pages 26-29) she has performed the role of the landscape architect in unifying a project comprising four apartment buildings by very different architects, while creating places of richness of space and form.

Pattern can be used to recall a site's history, as George Hargreaves has done with the braided stream at the University of Cincinnati (pages 32-35). Hargreaves has been known as a pattern maker since he designed the black-and-white square patterned Harlequin Plaza in Englewood, Colorado (1985). The Cincinnati project is not just about pattern. It is also the story of a site being reclaimed from the motorcar, the creation of campus recreation areas and of a landscape architect's long-term commitment - Hargreaves has been working at the University of Cincinnati since 1989.

In Mito City, Japan (pages 36-39) Shodo Suzuki has patterned his site with grand geometrical forms: the circle, the triangle and the square. He has created a place that he terms a People's Plaza, with patterns that can be experienced from several storeys above as well as at ground level. The use of pattern and geometrical shapes here relates to Eastern Cosmology and in particular the five basic elements: earth, water, fire, wind and air as represented by geometry. By contrast, at the NTT Headquarters in Tokyo (pages 40-43) Diana Balmori has played with a square grid, which transmutes from hard pavement to soft parterre and which is part of a larger play with materials. Here the pattern is part of the intellectual structure of the design.

The desire for consistency and to create a framework informs Jeppe Aagaard Andersen's approach at Ørestad in Denmark (pages 44-45) where he has used simple tree grids to control future development. The challenge for Andersen is that the new town is development-led and therefore coherence has to come from the landscape design. This is expressed in the road and rail infrastructure that provides the links that hold this new town together.

At Hattersheim in Germany (pages 18-21) Herbert Dreiseitl is operating at the smaller end of the urban design scale. His real accomplishment is to do with urban ecology and introducing living water into his projects, but here he also used grid-patterned paving in the Market Place to hold the design together: the water, whether in the form of a water course or flowform scupture, then contrasts with the paving grid pattern.

But pattern need not be primarily hard paving. At Mas de los Voltes (pages 14-17) Fernando Caruncho uses fields framed by avenue planting to pattern his *ferme ornée*. Here, the pattern is formed of living plant materials: crops, grass and lines of olive and cypress trees. This a scheme where the pattern changes through the seasons as crops grow, are harvested and the land is ploughed again.

Endnotes
1 *Shorter Oxford English Dictionary* (Oxford, Clarendon Press, 1944)
2 Dorothy Stroud, in *Capability Brown* (London, Faber and Faber, 1975, p.157) quotes Brown's letter of 1775 to the Rev. Thomas Dyer of Marylebone '...Place-making, and a good English Garden, depend intirely [sic] upon Principle and have very little to do with Fashion.'
3 Peter Walker: *Minimalist Gardens* (Washington DC, Spacemaker Press, 1997, p.17)

Mas de los Voltes
Ampurdán, Catalonia, Spain, 1995
Fernando Caruncho

In a project that leaps the bounds of gardening and becomes design in the landscape, Caruncho has produced a twentieth-century *ferme ornée*. He has carved, shaped and marked the landscape by lines of cypress (*Cupressus sempervirens*) alternating with olive trees within a setting of fields of wheat.

Ampurdán is in Catalonia, near the French border, and so this is a very green part of Spain. The design – a grid of plots defined by row trees – is typical of Caruncho. Grass paths penetrate the estate, and walks are placed between the wheat fields. The house itself is a *mas*, a farmhouse, and the walks and views reach into the fields rather than leading to wider vistas beyond. There are no eye-catchers or landmarks on the horizon, but rather, the grid is internally generated.

The house is elevated on a slope, and there are wide terraced steps down to the first feature, a set of four square, brick-edged basins with wide grass walks between. These basins are set within a vineyard. This is a landscape design that grabs the sky – reflected in the basins – rather than connecting with the wider landscape around. To the north there is another brick-edged basin, this one circular and standing alone. With its limpid reflection of the row trees it provides the perfect destination for a circuit walk.

'Ornamented farm' this may be, but it has a simplicity and almost minimalist purity that is very much of the late twentieth century. What is particularly remarkable is the contrast between the mown grass paths and the enclosing fields of wheat, which as the months pass become fields of brown ploughed earth. Caruncho describes the changing seasons: 'In the summer, the wheat is tall and golden and the great plots sway gently in the wind. There is fruit in the orchard. Autumn brings the grape harvest and the cutting of the wheat. In winter the earth is ploughed and sown and marked by wonderful patterns.' In this way, enclosure leads to exposure.

Caruncho studied philosophy at university, and it is the Greek sense of the continuity of man and nature that appeals to him. His expression of nature is through the use of the grid: he sees in its regular geometry a way of conveying something human and unchanged. As he puts it, 'Since the Neolithic Age, man has tirelessly repeated the same patterns on everything from pottery to weaving.'

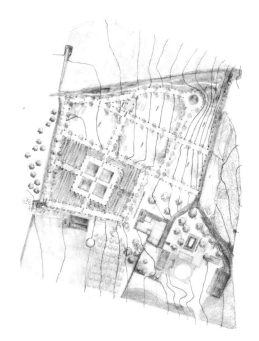

Above: Plan of the landscape garden, showing the *mas* at bottom right, the vineyard to the left, the four square pools in the centre and a great triangle of five wheat fields at the top, with paths leading to the circular pool.

Right: Grass path, brick edge, olive tree and wheat, with dark woodland beyond: this is a design that plays with the changes in light and colour throughout the agricultural year.

Above: The Mas de los Voltes farmhouse is set in the wooded Catalan landscape.

Above: The allées of cypress and olive trees throw alternating patterns of shadow onto the mown grass paths and the ploughed fields.

Right: Old olive trees such as these are a staple of the Mediterranean landscape. They also evoke Caruncho's favoured historical references, to Ancient Greek philosophy and Mediterranean civilization.

Above: Looking across the landscape garden from the circular basin towards the farmhouse, or *mas*. This is a walk that leads to both house and vineyard.

Right: A similar view at evening time, showing how the light has changed.

Above and right: An avenue
of sharply pointed
cypresses marches across
the fields, their even spread
contrasting with the
apparent irregularity of the
woodland trees.

Market Place and Water Steps
Hattersheim, Hesse, Germany, 1988-93
Atelier Dreiseitl

Herbert Dreiseitl's classic scheme of urban placemaking and hydrological design from the 1990s brings water right into the centre of Hattersheim, a small town just south-west of Frankfurt. The *Marktplatz* and *Wassertreppe* (market place and water steps) scheme arose out of a competition that took place in 1988, which Dreiseitl won in conjunction with Walter Architects from Wiesbaden. Recycled, clean water is the link through all the elements of the scheme.

The path of the recycled rainwater starts from the top of the steps outside the old post office and town hall. From here it descends through a series of basins that have been sculpted into a flowform waterfall, which appears to grow out of the granite steps. At the base of the steps it takes the form of a shallow rill to cross the market place. The market place itself is paved with a 5 metre (16 foot) square grid of lines of red, engineering brick laid on edge with dark granite and basalt setts, and white quartz setts within the brick circles at the junctions of each square. The water passes through three shallow linked basins, the channel curving around the straight edge of the paving grid and enfolding three trees before disappearing and then re-emerging on the far side of the market place at the edge of the town centre park. Here the rainwater becomes a meandering naturalized stream and ends in a reed-bordered pool with a fountain. Finally, a 1.2 kilowatt pump re-circulates the water, which has a total volume of 2,000 cubic metres (2,614 cubic yards).

Herbert Dreiseitl's interest is both in people and in natural processes. 'People must be given the opportunity to experience water again', he says. 'Water resources can only become sustainable when social values grant water the necessary priority.' He quotes three particular influences: the flowform sculptures of the English artist John Wilkes; Theodore Schwenk, a hydrologist who studied the forms and rhythms of water movement; and the carpenter-cum-philosopher-cum-educationalist, Hugo Kükelhaus.

The Atelier Dreiseitl group comprises between 20 and 25 people. It currently includes seven landscape architects; a water technologist; two civil engineers and a model-maker. Work takes place in a crafts workshop rather than in a landscape architect's office: the Dreiseitl team is based in a former factory in Überlingen, where they use both models and computer simulation. For the Hattersheim project the water basins and steps were designed using life-size clay models.

According to Dreiseitl, 'natural flow patterns are always paired with great beauty', while 'drainage pattern illustrates the slowness of the process'. At Hattersheim, the design illustrates a natural process by modelling its patterns.

Above: The granite water steps under construction.

Right: Water is a natural medium for play.

Top right: Flowform basins and red granite steps bring fresh water into the centre of this small town.

Opposite: The steps below the old post office and town hall are sculpted into a flowform waterfall. Recycled water cascades down to the market place, with its striking gridded paving. Along one side of the square are situated a bistro, bar and pizzeria with plenty of outdoor seating, just visible at the left edge of this picture.

Left: Rough granite paving slabs provide a safe non-slip crossing for all.

Above: In the park, the retention pool – complete with fountain, reeds and irises – forms the end of the circuit. From here a pump re-circulates the water. The pool is encircled by simple bound macadam with granite-slab stepping stones.

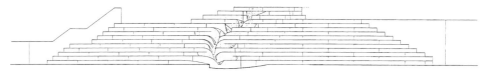

Above left: Towards the pool, the watercourse becomes planted and naturalized.

Above right: Water meanders through the park, with the market square in the distance.

Top right: The key elements of the market square. Solid granite steps are sculpted into flowform basins which lead down to a brick-edged rill. Note the specially designed manhole cover.

Above: Elevation of the steps, which were designed by modelling rather than drawing.

Right: Detail of the flowform steps which help to aerate the recycled water.

Sony Complex

Potsdamer Platz, Berlin, Germany, 1992-2000
Peter Walker, William Johnson and Partners

The Sony Complex was one of the first developments to begin after Berlin's reunification, when the American architect Helmut Jahn won the competition in 1992. The developers – a joint venture comprising the Sony Corporation, Tishman Speyer Properties and Kajima Corporation – had bought the land from the City of Berlin. The former wasteland site, which was bisected by the Berlin Wall, is now set to reclaim its pre-War role as the centre of Berlin's nightlife. Originally the City stipulated that the developers keep to the old street blocks and that buildings should not exceed 35 metres (115 feet) in height to be consonant with the historic pattern of Berlin's streets. Sony agreed as part of the deal to build a permanent home for the German Filmhaus and to lease it out at a low rent.

However, essentially this is a very commercial property development providing 132,500 square metres (1.4 million square feet) of gross floor space.

The 2.5 hectare (6 ½ acre) Sony site occupies a triangle with an apex on Potsdamer Platz itself and lies between Bellevuestrasse, Entlastungsstrasse and Potsdamerstrasse and extends to Kemperplatz, where it meets the Tiergarten.

At the centre of this plot is the Forum, which is surrounded by five 12-storey buildings, while five other buildings face the outer street sides of the triangle. The masterplanners Murphy/Jahn have opened up the traditional Berlin block form and connected the usual introverted internal courtyard to the outside world. At the same time they have created an internal sweep of pedestrian streets with the lozenge-shaped Forum – a major public space – at the centre. There is another smaller piazza alongside the 24-storey curved office tower. The buildings sing transparently with light at night. The Forum is 100 metres (328 feet) across and covered with a hyperbolic cone of PTFE (polytetrafluoroethylene) glass fibre membrane strips alternating with laminated glass to create a huge internal piazza, flooded with striped sunlight. The 11-storey high space is filled with people walking to the U-Bahn station, patronizing the street-level restaurants, and passing by in a state of 'osmotic synergy' with city life outside.

Sony's eight-storey European headquarters is at the northern Kemperplatz apex, while on Bellevuestrasse sit a residential development and the rebuilt Grand Hotel Esplanade, into which the surviving Kaiser's Room was incorporated as a restaurant. Sony used its muscle to persuade the City to accept Jahn's scheme, which rose far too high, broke the rules, and generally defied expectations.

Peter Walker's landscape scheme exploits the exploded city block form and celebrates the overlap of public and private realm. Large granite paving slabs – familiar elements in the Berlin city scene – cover the ground and are contrasted by perforated inlays of aluminium panels, which act as drainage gratings and allow freedom in the placement of trees. The floor of the Forum is composed of a series of layers, which rise or open to reveal elements beneath. The circular pool at the centre is partially cantilevered as a glass disc over the cinema's lower level, projecting ripples and letting natural light flood the area underneath.

Light is also used to unify the site in the form of strips of glass set diagonally into the pavement which are illuminated by fibreoptics at night. Stainless-steel furniture and allées of row trees are also used throughout to lend a sense of unity. In response to the Centre's rule-breaking architectural scheme Walker celebrates the site's modulation between old Berlin, with its rigid urban block structure and granite, and Jahn's high-tech vision of a modern city.

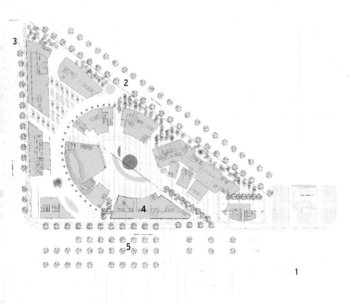

Above: The traditional introverted Berlin city block has been opened out and connected to the wider city as a public place. At the centre of this plot is the covered Forum. The streets are located on the plan as follows:

1. Potsdamer Platz
2. Bellevuestrasse
3. Entlastungsstrasse
4. Filmhaus
5. Neue Potsdamerstrasse

Above: Stainless steel – a Peter Walker trademark – is used for street furniture.

Left: Allées of row trees and stainless-steel benches are used throughout to lend the scheme a visual unity.

Above: The theme of circles and semi-circles is set by the pool and the adjacent planted area. Typical Berlin granite paving slab is inlaid with lines of perforated aluminium sheeting and diagonal lines of glass; fibreoptics light these at night.

Overleaf: Sunlight through the tensile roof structure creates an ever-changing pattern on the Forum floor, and filters through the glass section of the pool to project rippling effects on the level below.

Kitagata Apartments

Kitagata, Gifu Prefecture, Japan, 2000
Martha Schwartz

The Kitagata Public Housing Project began as an idea by Arata Isozaki and as an experiment in social housing supported by the Governer of Gifu Prefecture, Taju Kajiwara. Kitagata is mid-way between Tokyo and Osaka on Honshu Island. At Isozaki's instigation, four female architects – Akiko Takahashi, Kazuyo Sejima, Christine Hawley and Elizabeth Diller – were each asked to design a separate apartment block for an ideal site. Each was encouraged to design in isolation. Continuity came from the landscape architect, Martha Schwartz, while Isozaki, the one male architect involved, acted as masterplanner.

The architects developed their different approaches within the brief for four ten-storey high blocks containing single-person apartments. The building footprints vary: Takahashi's is straight, Diller's slightly curved, Hawley's L-shaped, and Sejima's zig-zagged. These shapes create spatial widenings off the main strip. The four apartment blocks are distributed to create a continuous, long east-west space between the ten-storey blocks. An east-west space like this is of course shaded for most of the day on the south side (Schwartz was not asked to ignore the site) and sunlit on the north. She has moderated the outside face of the scheme by planting lines of row trees. The site was a green paddy field and the idea of dykes and paddy fields suggested the scheme of sunken garden rooms accommodating active and quiet play. Within the great communal space she has created compartment gardens – a place where ground patterning is very visible from the medium-rise apartments around.

The long courtyard is divided in the middle by one north-south road running between the four blocks. Straddling this is the Willow Court with its still pools. There are three linear features arranged east-west: the Iris Canal, the Bamboo Garden and a rill. The other enclosed gardens are set out with a mix of passive and active spaces. The American critic Marc Treib has likened this to an Italianate garden.

To the west are the Cherry and Willow Gardens, linked by the Iris Canal, and also a dance floor and play space. To the east is the other Willow Garden and the Stone and Bamboo Gardens, sports area, the rill and the small gardens of the Four Seasons. All these compartments and features are set out on a raised field of gravel, subdivided by lines of fastigiate trees, which meets a simple black-and-white patterned paved parking area along the shady south side. On the north side there is a similar pattern of spaces subdivided by row trees, from which a rock-studded curved stone wall rises up to the gravel area and the Cherry Garden. Schwartz likes to emphasize trees, and in this garden the cherries (*Prunus* sp.) are marked with random block-rubble circles raised above the level of the gravel.

Schwartz has always liked to play with landscape – her first widely known project was the Bagel Garden in Boston's Back Bay. Clients often do not understand that fun can also be serious. Here Schwartz appears to have found a client who has taken her seriously and in consequence the apartment dwellers of Kitagata can enjoy in full the results of a light, lively and always life-enhancing landscape designer.

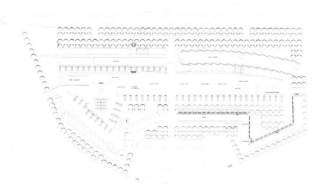

Above: Site plan: the different gardens are shown in the middle black area, with the apartment blocks above and below.

Top right: View of the Cherry Garden from the north-west block with the Iris Canal beyond. On either side of the road across the gardens are the Willow Water Gardens.

Right: The view over the illuminated Four Seasons Gardens at dusk with the patterned parking area in the foreground.

Above: The Four Seasons
Gardens – Red, Green,
Yellow and Blue – with the
Bamboo Garden beyond.

Right: The illuminated
Plexiglas screens of the
Four Seasons Gardens sing
at night.

Top: The Cherry Garden. The trees, surrounded by random stone paving circles, the rough-rock studded curved wall and simple paving patterns give this area a sense of grandeur.

Above left: The sunken play area.

Above right: The stone garden appears to be made of pink rock candy.

Opposite, top: The western Willow Garden. The shallow water, tree islands, underwater uplighters and willow trees on a simple square grid provide a cool, calm resting area. In time the willows will mature and offer more shade.

Opposite, below: A detailed garden plan. The elements are, from left to right: 1. Cherry Garden, 2. Iris Canal, 3. Dance Floor, 4. Play area, 5. Willow Garden, 6. Stone Garden, 7. Sports area, 8. Bamboo Garden, 9. Rill and 10. Four Seasons Gardens.

Agnes Katz Plaza

Pittsburgh, Pennsylvania, USA, 1998

Dan Kiley

The project forms part of the Pittsburgh Cultural Trust's 14-block Downtown District Plan to bring cultural and environmental improvement to the city's Penn-Liberty area. When the Cultural Trust set up the plan in 1990 the area was mainly a red light district. Now it has parks and four refurbished theatres. The Agnes Katz Plaza project alone cost $4 million, of which half came from the Cultural Trust and half from the state. Of the Trust's $2 million contribution, half came from Marshall Katz, a member of the Cultural Trust's Board of Trustees, and Andrea Katz McCutcheon. The plaza is named in honour of their mother, Agnes R. Katz.

The small city plaza – just 2,000 square metres (15,000 square feet) – is located at the junction of Penn Avenue and Seventh Street, close to the Theater Square project by Michael Graves. The purpose of the plaza was to house a large Louise Bourgeois sculpture as well as a number of her 'eye' benches. So this is a place where we can see the work of two masters designing together. Initially the intention was to locate the large sculpture at the rear of the site (to take advantage of the backdrop of the high-rise Century Building behind), but later the designers chose a central location to allow free circulation around the piece. The 7.5 metre (25 foot) high bronze sculpture rises as an essay of

ridges in the shape of a bifurcated cone out of a 100mm (4 inch) deep basin of water set on a lowered terrace. The surrounding pool edge mirrors the double cone effect. The pool is intentionally small so that viewers can get close to the sculpture. The water terrace is paved with 50mm (2 inch) granite setts and is sunk 450mm (18 inches) below the level of the surrounding paving, so that the sculpture seems to rise out of the paving around it like an iceberg. From the street the space appears to flow across the place uninterrupted, but once inside the visitor is aware of being in a separate, lower space.

On the Penn Avenue frontage Bourgeois's granite 'eyeball' pieces rise abruptly out of the paving. This is a landscape design of great simplicity, a modest space inhabited and made something extraordinary by one of America's greatest landscape architects of the twentieth century.

As Kiley writes: 'Our intent was to create a plaza of the utmost simplicity, a space that is a pleasing interlude from the city street, yet is an integral part of the urban circulation pattern.'

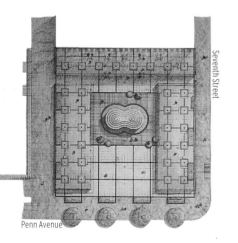

Seventh Street

Penn Avenue

Above: This is a direct use of urban space, defined in Kiley's classic gridded style – in this case symmetrical and composed with row trees.

Right: Bourgeois's granite eyeball benches are preludes to the folds of the large ridged double cone, the centrepiece of the plaza.

Top right: The view from above looking towards Penn Avenue with the Louise Bourgeois sculpture in the centre.

Above: The apparently random placement of the three pairs of granite eyeballs is complemented by Kiley's strictly symmetrical grid. The backdrop is the Century Building, which Kiley intends to be clad in ivy.

Right: At night the plaza and the sculptures are lit, creating a sense of outdoor urban theatre.

Campus Green

University of Cincinnatti, Ohio, USA, 1989-2000

George Hargreaves Associates

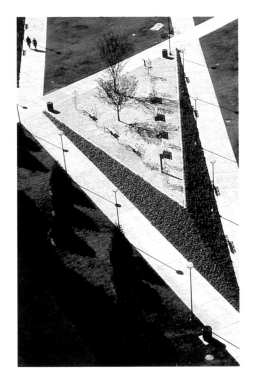

George Hargeaves has been masterplanning the University of Cincinatti since 1989. He has identified force fields - axial lines - which link the university's open spaces and he allowed for 185,000 square metres (2 million square feet) of new building development. He has reinforced the university's existing campus quadrangles and introduced the character of the adjacent Burnet Woods. Finally, he has begun to establish links between the original West Campus (where the university was founded in 1819) and the more recent East Campus. The East and West campuses are like two squares touching at a corner, and Campus Green is the north-eastern corner of the West Campus. In providing this link between the campuses, Hargreaves has re-established the pre-eminence of the pedestrian.

Campus Green - a 2.4 hectare (6 acre) open space - was formerly a large parking lot. Now there are open lawns, gardens, a sculpture garden and an arboretum. The site was once crossed by a stream, and so to recall that origin the design lays new curving, streamlike paths like a braid over the straight geometry of the force fields. The former parking lot has become the social centre of the campus and now accommodates a bookshop, Alumni and Faculty centres, the College of Business and student housing.

In essence the design comprises a set of extensive lawns with three main features. First, there is an international arboretum and associated earthworks - international in the sense that it includes species that have a worldwide distribution such as black cherry (*Prunus serotina*) and apple (*Malus sp.*). Second, there is the conical mount with water stairs built of the local limestone, a major landmark. Emerging from the mount there is a curving wall marking the entrance to the campus from the north. To commemorate the old stream there is a new stream

consisting of a stone runnel into which surface water run-off is fed. The third feature of the design comprises three raised triangular gardens with flowering trees to provide a place of peace and quiet within Campus Green. Hargreaves describes the development of the masterplan in this way: '*The first of the open spaces we created was McKicken Commons. It's a simple, green quad formed by the campus's most historic buildings. Then we went on to what we call object-spaces - Library Square and Sigma Sigma Amphitheater - where the open space functions like a building façade. Library Square, which is primarily paved, is about the unfolding of knowledge, embodied in a spiral. Sigma Sigma Amphitheater is a convocation space for students, faculty and alumni and its message is expressed through a light tower. With Campus Green, we return to the theme of the quadrangle - only this time, the quad has been folded in a couple of times, so that other themes come into play. They give Campus Green more character than simply a green space with some trees.*'

George Hargreaves is Professor and Chairman of Landscape Architecture at Harvard, and it shows. There is in his work the idea of a long-term commitment to place, an intellectual development, and an exploration of the ideas of land re-use and what he terms 'connection'. Those who work in universities know the ignorance and arrogance exhibited by some academics and managers. At Cincinnati the university is fortunate to be led by those who have confidence in what a gifted landscape architect can do: appreciate the site, realize its potential, and do so with great intellectual coherence and panache. Of the transformation of parking lot into campus, Hargreaves says: 'Our work acknowledges the simple truth that "made" landscapes can never be natural. With increasing frequency our work deals with land which has been made and re-made.'

Above: Raised triangular gardens provide a respite from the flurry of movement and meetings, though of course there are internet connections for laptops by the benches for those wanting to maintain links with the outside world.

Top: View from the north-east with the landmark cone to the near right and the braided footpaths clearly visible to the left.

The braided network of paths recalls the stream system that once ran through here. On the far right is the curve of the surface water runnel system, which, after rains, brings the stream back to life again. The raised earthworks recall Native American serpent mounds.

Left: A stretch of the
surface water drainage
system in the campus lawn.

Above: When experienced at
ground level the elements of
the drainage runnel, the
serpentine mounds and the
braided paving come
together.

Above: The large conical mount is a major feature and like a Tudor garden mount provides a point from which to view the whole green.

Right: The conical mount as seen when commissioned from ground level.

Ibaraki Prefecture Government Offices
Mito City, Japan, 1994-2000
Shodo Suzuki

Shodo Suzuki is known for his love of stone and of geometrical form and line. As he puts it, 'horizontal and vertical lines and surfaces based on perpendicular lines, oblique lines, and circles, squares and triangles, parabolae, circular arcs, and revolutions are preferable to the conventional freehand straight line used in the eighteenth and nineteenth century.' At the Ibaraki Prefecture he has translated this into a dialogue between the natural and the artificial, the new and the old.

The 120 metre (393 foot) high main building was designed by the architects Matsuda-Hirata and houses a regional assembly, government offices and police headquarters on a 15 hectare (37 acre) site. Previously the site was a Department of Forestry and Fisheries breeding station, and existing pine trees from the site were transplanted to the periphery of the new landscape design. The inner areas, on the other hand, are planted with deciduous trees to emphasize seasonal change. The old site also had a moat and this has been recalled in the new design.

The road approach is on axis to the main entrance and rises up out of a cutting to become an avenue which then runs under the Citizen's Plaza, a great silver-grey stone circle in front of the main entrance. This circle has two segments of curved shelters on either side of the approach axis and a circular shaft, like a ring of steel, which allows light into the parking level below. The circle is divided into six and patterned in different shades of white, grey and black stone forming striped patterns at 45 degree angles to the radii. The effect is austere and rigorous.

To left and right of the circular entrance court is a giant roof garden located over the parking and service areas. This roof garden comprises grass squares from which rise roof lights

and ventilation shafts as simple geometrical forms contrasting with the green. On both sides there are subsidiary stone areas, one a triangle and the other a square. Both are patterned in stripes like the central circle. Rows of trees connect these forms to the roof garden. Between the wings of the office building there are also lower level subsidiary spaces, which are primarily paved.

Local stone from Ibaraki is a theme throughout both the building and landscape design. Inada-ishi and Makabe-ishi granites were used for the outer walls and floors of the buildings, while local Kansuiseki marble was used for the walls of the prefecture assembly building.

The use of pattern and geometrical shapes relates to Eastern Cosmology and represents the five basic elements: earth, water, fire, wind and air. The triangle (*sankaku*) represents fire, the circle or globe (*en*) represent water, and the square (*ho*) represents the earth.

Further out beyond the level of the roof deck the grounds become a public park and are much more recognizable as the work of Suzuki at his more usual scale. The stones are rougher hewn and form terrace walls out of large Aztec-sized blocks and lines of paving in the grass. There are also rather stiffly shaped pools and canals with curved corners and turnings. The planted effects are extremely simple: there are lush green lawns of long grass and trees are planted either in rows or as coppices. The intention has been to represent the natural woodland and lake landscape of Ibaraki Prefecture. A straight-lined path around the perimeter has the effect of a frame, particularly when viewed from the offices above. However, it is when one comes right up close to the stone terraces and the megaliths that one sees Suzuki at his most characteristic.

Above: The subsidiary square is cut across by trees and planted in one corner. To the right a segment is open to the parking area beneath.

Right: With its terraced stone retaining walls the entrance road is an exercise in directional linearity.

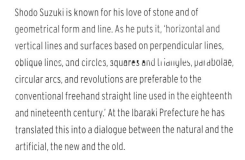

Top: View from the office building showing the approach road (top) rising from its cutting and then disappearing below the patterned stone Citizen's Plaza (bottom).

Above: The circular Citizen's Plaza in front of the main entrance. According to Suzuki 'the circle is the symbol for the *satori* or spiritual awakening.'

Right: The circular steel shaft allows light to penetrate the level below the Citizen's Plaza, highlighting Suzuki's simple geometrical sculpted forms.

Top three pictures: In the parkland areas Suzuki's design becomes less geometrical and the hard effects of the stone are countered by water and grass. Sometimes (as above) the grass and paving are interwoven.

Left: Aerial view of the park, which is framed by the perimeter path.

Monoliths in the public park. 'Horizontals and verticals are something I try to keep very much in mind whenever using stones... however complicated the shape of a stone is, it still has a centre of gravity and in order to give it a sense of stability the very core of that stone must be on a vertical in line with its centre of gravity.' (Shodo Suzuki)

NTT Headquarters
Shinjuku-ku, Tokyo, Japan, 1995
Balmori Associates

Nippon Telephone and Telegraph headquarters is a 7,229 square metre (78,899 square foot) site in Tokyo with two buildings by Cesar Pelli (with whom Diana Balmori of Balmori Associates used to work). Each building is a segment of a circle: the tallest is a 30-storey high semicircle with telecommunications centre below, while the other is a smaller 90 degree wedge. The two curved façades face each other, indeed the buildings almost touch and are connected by a covered way.

Across the site Balmori has drawn two sets of parallel pairs of lines (which cross each other in a plaid pattern) in wide bands of grey tiles. Near the building she has laid a fine buff-coloured bound macadam between the lines of the tiles and away from the buildings she has laid grass lawns. The circular shape of the smaller building is continued round and marked by an enclosure to create a corral, which defines the inner private space from the outer public area. The enclosure could be called a fence, but this is a transforming fence. It is made of cedar posts with a square grid of slats in between but the slats change from flat stainless steel to rounded timber. This is a fence where intellectual games are being played, where materials are used as metaphors for technology and nature.

The line of the curved fence is repeated within by a raised curved water channel in concrete which begins at a glazed steel water chute and ends in a sort of large empty concrete plug hole. The bed of the channel is in ridged steel to create eddying patterns in the water. Two bridges rise to cross the channel - one is in wood but with metal stepping stones at the point of crossing and the other is steel. The main space faces eastwards and becomes increasingly covered in trees the further one moves away from the buildings. Outside the corral Balmori has used evergreen Camphor trees

(*Cinnamomum camphora*), and inside she has planted deciduous maples (*Acer* sp.).

According to Balmori the design is based on two themes: the use of land, and the relationship between art and nature. The land use theme was driven by the functional need to house a monthly technological fair and by Tokyo's need for parks and open spaces. The theme of the relationship between art and nature is expressed through the materials and work processes used. The strategic use of timber and metal highlights the relationship between nature and technology. Natural patterns are created in the water using artificially made ridges. This theme is illustrated by Balmori's original intention to use natural wind energy to power an obviously man-made fountain (unfortunately in the end an electric pump was substituted for windpower). As Balmori explains it:

At NTT I tried to show the steps from nature to a highly technological aesthetic as a series of steps that move away from but keep a relationship with nature... in the changing design of the fence... At one end the fence is surrounded by trunks of evergreen trees and itself is made of trunk-like logs. As the fence moves towards the Museum of Technology, it remains a wood fence, however the wood is not cylindrical but flat and it becomes mixed with stainless steel. Then it becomes stainless steel completely. Stainless steel is iron ore and carbon. It is a much more processed material than the trunk...

Balmori is an intellectually challenging landscape designer. She teaches at Yale University, writes extensively and lectures. She is also an exhibiting photographer. The NTT project is unmistakably the work of a scholar and thinker.

Above: The transforming fence in its stainless steel phase, flattened and very processed.

Right: The same fence now in timber with, rounded posts and natural wood.

Top right: The ramped steel bridge, which crosses the water channel.

Opposite: The curved water channel in the private area, with the plug hole outlet at the bottom and one of the bridges at the centre, this version being in timber. The strong banding of the paving is still visible when seen from thirty floors up.

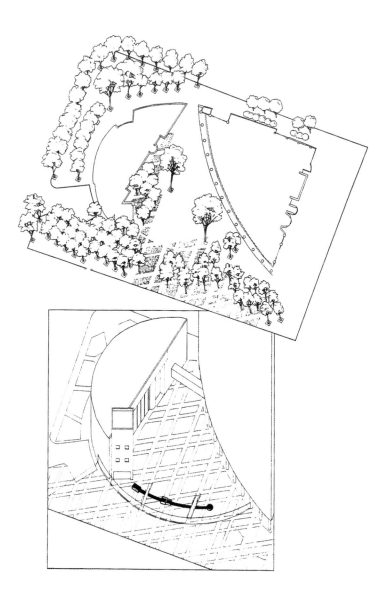

Top left: Axonometric drawings showing the paving (bottom) and vegetation layers (top) of the landscape design.

Left: The timber bridge is interrupted by stepping stones at the point of crossing.

Above: The curved 30-
storey façade of the
███████████ ████████
approached across a paved
and patterned landscape
garden. The hard, processed
design of this area echoes
the technological nature of
the business inside.

Ørestad

Amager Island, Copenhagen, Denmark, 1995-
Jeppe Aagaard Andersen

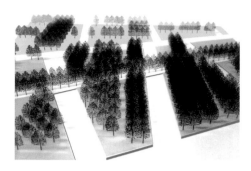

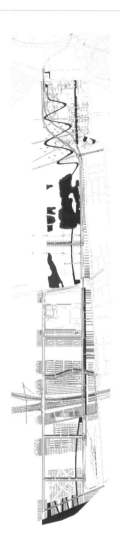

The new town of Ørestad is being developed south of Copenhagen on Amager Island. The town has road links to the new Øresund bridge which connects Denmark to Sweden, and thanks to the bridge the area is at the centre of a fast developing region between Copenhagen and Malmö. The new town is also linked to Copenhagen by metro – there is no need for big public plazas because people are constantly on the move. To the north is Copenhagen centre and to the east there is a largely built-up area leading to Copenhagen Kastrup Airport. The new town extends from the university campus to the north to just south of the E20 motorway, which crosses the island from west to east and then continues across the bridge to Sweden. Therefore, Amager Island is ideally situated for development as an outlet for commercial pressures placed on the area by the airport and the Øresund link. The project is managed by the Ørestad Development Corporation, which is jointly owned by the City of Copenhagen and the Kingdom of Denmark.

The new town takes the form of a long north-south strip or belt, 600 metres (1,968 feet) wide and five kilometres (three miles) long and covering 310 hectares (765 acres) in the centre of the island. Western Amager Island is composed mainly of old salt marsh with some landfill. Development guidelines stipulate that 100 hectares (247 acres) must not be built upon and that of the 200 hectares (494 acres) remaining, 60 per cent should be for commercial use, 20 per cent for housing, and 20 per cent for trade and cultural uses. The housing is intended to accommodate 20,000 people. From 1994 to 1995 a competition was held, which was won by the Finnish firm ARKKI. The Danish landscape architect Jeppe Aagaard Andersen was then appointed in 1998.

The plan of the landscape hinges on a water system and a canal, which is closely followed by the new metro line. This is very much a wild, flat polder type of site, which is open and exposed but with a rich flora. The development is intended to take up to 30 years. The original plan was to plant the whole site with 10, 682 mature trees to provide an instant forest effect. The trees were to be planted on a grid so that the development could then be carved out of the trees. In fact events have overtaken the original plans and development is proceeding anyway.

However, the hand of the landscape architect is still to be seen in the consistency of detailing, the use of granite and the control of the main public spaces, which are the metro line, the road highway system and finally the water network. The whole development, which is quite intense, is offset by the adjacent marsh and heathland areas of Amager that lie to the west. The landscape architect has had the challenging task of dealing with the enormous commercial pressures of the development while at the same time maintaining a sense of coherence.

Above: Plan showing the waterway in blue and planting in green.

Top right: The original model reflects Andersen's plan to plant large numbers of trees on a grid pattern.

Right: This map of the Øresund area shows how well-placed Ørestad is on the new link route between Copenhagen and Malmö. Amager Island is on the left of the map, south-east of Copenhagen.

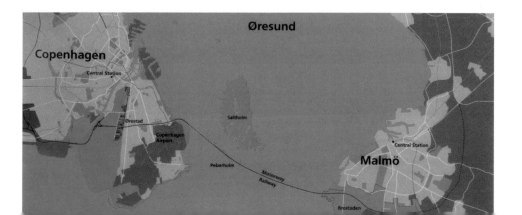

Above: the waterway is one aspect of the landscape design that will help to control the nature of future development.

Right: Aerial views of the town (left) and the surrounding marsh area (right).

chapter 2 minimalism

The term minimalism is associated with 'impersonal austerity, plain geometric configurations and industrially processed materials'.[1] For art historians Minimalism is a movement which began in the 1960s with the austere work of Americans Donald Judd and Carl Andre at the Chinati Foundation in Marfa, Texas. For architectural critics, Minimalism is a term that has been associated since the 1980s with such architects as John Pawson in the UK and the likes of Herzog and De Meuron in Switzerland, as well as with many Japanese architects who are working within their national architectural tradition (for example Kengo Kuma, whose museum at Nasu (pages 60-63) is illustrated here). For landscape architecture the term can be applied in a very literal way. Minimalist landscapes are unornamented and establish a functional frame for reaction and response.

Of course, this can produce something close to pattern-making - indeed, the definitions in this book do sometimes overlap, and should not be seen as exclusive. This is obvious at Tramvia Park (pages 48-51) where it is the pattern-making that gives the immediate impression. What is interesting about this scheme, however, is the avowed expression of the motorway function underneath it. A comparable approach to the process of design is seen at Adriaan Geuze's Borneo scheme in Amsterdam (pages 52-55) where again his own design work (for instance the bridges) is far from minimalistic. But at Borneo there is an 'impersonal austerity' and a use of 'plain geometric configurations' in his establishment of development guidelines for the different architects. Such control requires an admirable rigour. What is really exciting at Borneo is that the place changes as it is populated, because this is a place that has been designed to change in a way which is almost organic.

Such urban choreography can also be seen at Rådhusplads in Copenhagen (pages 56-59) where the design itself becomes a backdrop to the movement of people, and to the urban scene of traffic and buildings, both by day and, most especially, at night. Something of the same is also seen at Whileinch in Glasgow (pages 68-71), where Gross Max have made a place out of a corner plot using simple elements, or on a larger scale at Enschede Station (pages 72-75) where OKRA have used materials and forms in a simple and austere way.

Minimalism can also be applied to the landscape of commerce as at the Matchworks in Liverpool (pages 76-79) where materials are used simply and functionally to compose spaces and circulation in that most soulless of situations, the car-dominated 'business village'. The architects, however, also make reference to the site's history and thus tell a story.

At the Parc de la Théols in Issoudun (pages 64-67), Desvigne and Dalnoky have applied minimalism to a rural site. Here they have taken the elements of the original field plot lines and composed a rural park. Then they have used simple vegetation forms, notably a restricted vocabulary of monospecific willow tree and shrub planting, to develop their scheme.

Endnotes
1 Jane Turner, ed.:
The Dictionary of Art
(New York and London,
Grove Dictionaries Inc.,
1996, vol. 21, p. 645)

Tramvia Park
Tiana-Montgat, Catalonia, Spain, 1999-2001
Batlle i Roig

When the A19 motorway was built north-east of Barcelona it divided the town of Tiana on the slopes of the hills above it from the coastal communities of Montgat and Turc de Montgat Montsolis. Named after the old Montgat-Tiana tramline, which linked the two settlements before its closure in 1955, a new linear park reconnects and serves these communities.

The site's problem was also the solution. The section of the road that is now covered by the park was mostly situated in a cutting which was divisive, but which could be covered as a tunnel, allowing the creation of a roof garden on top. Some sections of the motorway under the park emerge from the cutting, and in these areas the park above is supported by retaining walls. At a total width of 31.8 metres (100 feet), the park extends over 850 metres (2,788 feet) of the motorway. The architects understood that without irrigation (which would waste water) little in the way of grass or flowers would grow in the hot dry summers. The alternative was to produce a mainly hard and brightly coloured landscape.

The architects did not wish to hide or disguise the motorway tunnel underneath, but rather to celebrate it by emphasizing its line in the park's linear strip design, and by revealing the presence of the road in the vertical retaining walls where the road emerges from its cutting. The 6 hectare (15 acre) park consists of two strips. One strip echoes the motorway underneath in its use of brightly coloured macadam and precast concrete paving slabs. Above this there is a wider, green strip where the vegetation of the hillsides is being restored using indigenous trees, including *Robinia pseudoacacia*, *Jacaranda mimosifolia* and *Sophora japonica*. Benches and motorway-style streetlights make this park ideal for promenades or sports. This is a characteristically architectonic work in which imaginative architects have turned a problem into an asset.

Above: Once out from under the cover of the park the motorway reasserts its role of cutting a gash across the countryside.

Top and right: What would have been a division in the landscape has now become a linear park over the motorway. The geometric pattern of the retaining walls echoes that of the park's coloured, paved surface.

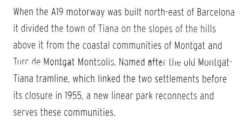

Opposite, top: The park comprises two strips: one the hard paved promenade and the other a green strip where the existing hillside landscape has been reinstated.

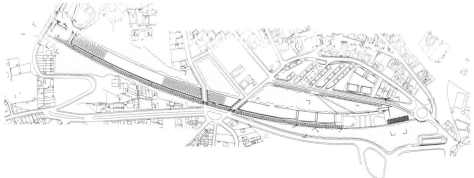

Left: The park extends 580 metres (2,788 feet) over the A19 motorway north-east of Barcelona. The yellow and black paved promenade strip is at the bottom of the park plan, with the wider planted strip above, and the entrance to the far left. The hill town of Tiana is to the north (top of plan), and the coastal community of Montgat to the south (bottom of plan).

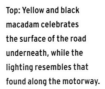

Top: Yellow and black macadam celebrates the surface of the road underneath, while the lighting resembles that found along the motorway.

Above and left: Views of the park entrance, built of geometrically patterned, warm red brickwork and cast concrete.

Above: The park acts as a promenade, with views of the hills when facing west (as in this image) and of the Mediterranean coast when facing east (see page 49).

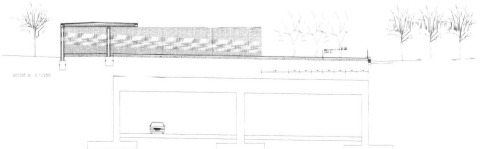

Left: Section through the
park entrance showing the

SECCIO B E 1/250

Borneo Sporenburg
Amsterdam, The Netherlands, 1993-7
West 8

Borneo and Sporenburg are the names of two quays in Amsterdam's nineteenth-century Eastern Docks. The docks were built on marshland (*rietlanden*) reclaimed from the River Ij as part of Amsterdam's great expansion beyond the canals of the seventeenth-century town centre. Developed in the 1870s to accommodate the East India trade following the opening of the North Sea Canal, the docks closed a century later. Each quay projects eastwards to embrace the Spoorwegbassin and face the reclaimed new town of Ijburg.

The Amsterdam Department of Physical Planning commissioned West 8 to produce a masterplan for the area in 1993. The brief was for 2,500 units of high-density low-rise housing, which equates with 100 units per hectare (41 units per acre) - three times the density of the average suburban housing. Of course the site also suggests water-related

activities. Landscape architect Adriaan Geuze of West 8 began by planning the building units. Effectively he designed guidelines for a variation on the traditional canal house inspired by the villages of the former Zuider Zee. The three-storey units, with patios and roof gardens, have ground floors with unusually high ceilings (3.5 metres/11 feet 6 inches rather than the Dutch norm of 2.4 metres/7 feet 10 inches) so that they can be converted into workshops, studio apartments or other types of spaces in future. The area is designed to be flexible, to allow a mixture of urban functions. The houses are built back to back with open-topped internal patios to ensure that light penetrates. This scheme is as much about allowing people the opportunity to develop their own private spaces as about public space. One parking space per building is allowed and cars can either be parked under the house, outside on the inner streets or in half-sunken parking garages. House plot depths are either 15, 17.5 or 19 metres (11 feet 6 inches, 19 feet or 20 feet 6 inches). A similar development brief was imposed on all types of dwellings be they expensive high-class units or social housing. Once these guidelines were established the masterplanner, West 8, handed over the building brief to more than 100 Dutch architects: each was to design one building. In addition to this, a double block of 100 house plots was sold directly to individual owners, avoiding the need for a developer. There are also three great housing blocks (Geuze refers to them as 'Meteorites') which act as landmarks. Located on Sporenburg are the apartment block The Whale (by Frits van Dongen) and Kees Christiaanse's 60 metre (197 foot) high Fountainhead

initially begun by American architect Steven Holl. On Borneo sits the Pacman apartment block designed by Koen van Velsen. The three blocks are aligned to three Amsterdam landmarks: the entrance to the Piet-Heintunnel, the axis of the Verbindingsdam and the Oranjesluizen (the great locks across the River Ij). The sculptural apartment buildings form new landmarks, and give the occupants spectacular views. The public space consists of streets 11 metres (36 feet) wide running east to west. There are also public green spaces diagonally arranged north to south, but the main public open spaces are along the docks and the river.

North-south access between the quays is also important and so West 8 (with a team comprising Geuze, Wim Kloosterboer and Yushi Uehara) have designed red steel Venetian-style bridges with stepped ramps which rise high above the water level (and also offer great views). Effectively this project is about creating an urban framework within which architects and buildings can operate, and consequently a setting for urban choreography. The spaces and the forms of the buildings are controlled, but within this framework games can be played and individual variety introduced - a variety that has allowed the streets and quaysides to become inhabited and alive.

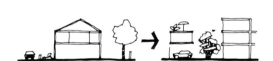

Above: The quays as they are today, after development: Borneo, at the bottom of the picture, is dominated by the Pacman building. The diagonal north-south cross-spaces and two of the red Venetian bridges can clearly be seen. Houseboats extend the habitable space.

Top right: A photograph looking west of the Eastern Docks before their closure: Borneo, covered in warehouses, is to the left and Sporenburg, with the railway yard, is to the right, with the Spoorwegbassin in between. Central Amsterdam is a 15-minute bicycle ride to the west.

Above left: A section of a typical Dutch suburban house (left) and the new low-rise, high-density canal house model (right).

Right: Canals and boats, access to water and views of the sky are what this scheme is about.

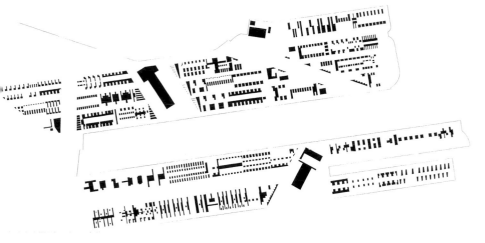

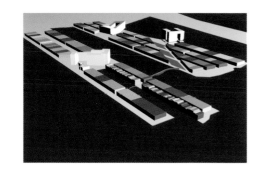

Above: Build your own house and have a boat mooring, as is the other on Borneo.

Top left: This roof plan, with built structures in black, reveals the surprising amount of private open space between and within the houses.

Top right: A model showing the organization of buildings, landmarks, monuments, connecting bridges and connecting open spaces. The three housing blocks can be clearly seen.

Right: Ground floor spaces, now used for parking or utility storage, can easily be converted into cafés workshops or galleries as owners' needs change.

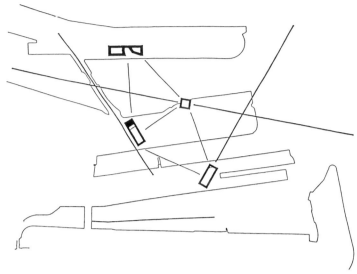

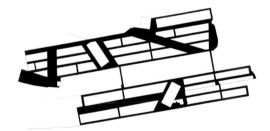

Top left: View down the large diagonal cross space on Sporenburg – the roof of The Whale building can be seen on the far left rising above the terraced housing.

Top right: Plan showing the arrangement of the viewlines and landmark buildings. Views run both between the landmark buildings and from the buildings westwards along the Verbindingsdam to the city centre and eastwards to Ijburg and the eastern tunnel mouths.

Above left: In this plan the open public spaces are represented in black. The streets are orientated east-west, while the major landmark buildings are orientated along the north-south connecting spaces.

Above centre: One of the inner 11 metre (36 foot) wide streets: the street is shaded for much of the time in winter due to its east-west orientation.

Above right: The quayside along the Spoorwegbassin: with people comes change and development.

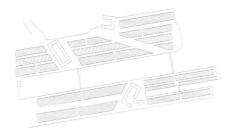

Above: The ownership plot diagram shows how direct and systematic this project is.

Top: Adriaan Geuze's big red Venetian-style bridges, which connect the quays, are Borneo's most characteristic design gesture. These bridges are fun to walk over and allow ease of navigation, but because they do not comply with Dutch disabled access regulations they were legally declared pieces of sculpture rather than bridges.

Above centre and right: The Whale apartment block by Fritz van Dongen of De Architect Compagnie dominates views of Sporenburg. The zinc-faced building occupies the same ground plan area as one of H.P. Berlage's 1920s Amsterdam housing blocks and consists of 214 apartments, with ground floor offices and basement parking.

Rådhusplads
Copenhagen, Denmark, 1979-95
KHR/AS Arkitekter

Rådhusplads is *the* place for great public celebrations and demonstrations in Copenhagen. From royal weddings and political demonstrations to the 1945 Victory parade, it is Copenhagen's Trafalgar Square or Place de la Bastille. Martin Nyrop's great brick City Hall and bell tower (completed 1905) dominate the square to produce an architectural composition reminiscent of the Piazza del Campo in Siena. Nyrop carried that inspiration further in his design for the square, which originally included a small cockleshell-shaped bowl – like that of the Piazza del Campo – facing the City Hall. In 1947, however, the square was repaved in granite. By the 1950s Rådhusplads was dominated by new shops, hotels and offices, and the original design gave way to a traffic intersection for trams, buses and cars.

The citizens of Copenhagen became unhappy with their once great city square and in 1979 a competition was organized for its redesign. The winning design, by KHR (Knud Holscher and Svend Axelsson) and traffic engineers Anders Nyvig A/S, was eventually completed in 1995, the year in which Copenhagen took its turn as European City of Culture. The new design involved a complete reorganization of traffic, including east-west links to Strøget, Copenhagen's main pedestrianized shopping street, and to Vesterbrogade, the street which leads to the main railway station and to Tivoli Gardens to the south. The unification of the two main pedestrian parts of the square was achieved by closing a portion of Vesterbrogade (although cyclists can still cross). Within this 6,000 square metre (21,000 square foot) pedestrian space there now exists a new and larger bowl-shaped depression, with a transport terminal and city information building. The bowl-shaped depression was achieved by raising the edges of the pedestrianized square, thus reducing the impact of the traffic around three sides.

To the south-west, the original Nyrop-designed balustrades and steps link the City Hall with the square, while to the north-west the terminal building is located beside a new bus terminus. Lines of maple (*Acer*) row trees reduce the impact of the buses in the terminal area and four horse chestnut trees (*Aesculus hippocastanum*) were placed at the southern end of the City Hall façade. Otherwise the square is unplanted.

The design is unshowy in its simplicity, featuring alternating bands of black granite and pre-cast concrete within the border of granite steps. In Copenhagen the design has been controversial precisely because it is so subdued. The form of the square is created by the buildings – the City Hall being the focus at one end and the terminal building – with its 60 metre (197 foot) long steel beam – elegantly and quite modestly provides a conclusion at the other. Traffic has not been excluded – it dominates the two long sides of the square, but no longer dominates the square itself. Indeed, the noise and bustle of traffic, especially at night, provide a cacophonous sense of excitement, enhanced by the illuminated façade of the Information Centre and the neon signs of the square's commercial buildings. Big city life is celebrated by a quiet and subtle design.

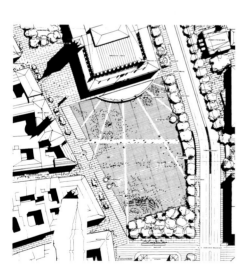

Above: KHR's 1980 layout plan: The Vester Voldgade roadway is on the left, where the Strøget feeds into the square, to the bottom right is the bus terminal, the City Hall is to the top and H.C. Andersens Boulevard runs along the far right.

Top right: The City Hall seen from the Information Centre across the square.

Above, The square from the north end, with the bus terminal to the left and the terminal building and Information Centre in the near foreground. Though the square does not exclude motor vehicles, pedestrians still have a feeling of ownership. The whole square is slightly tilted down to the front of the City Hall.

Right: The Information Centre at night. The illuminated windows follow the line of the Utrecht Building behind and on the far side of the bus station.

Above: View from the City
Hall steps across to the
Information Centre and
the Utrecht Building on
the far side of the square.
Pedestrians come first.

Right: Early sketch of
the view from the Vester
Voldgade where the
pedestrians from the
Strøget approach: the
sloped enclosure in
the drawing has since
become steps.

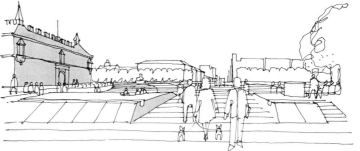

Right: Paving patterns are

Nasu History Museum
Nasu, Tochigi Prefecture, Japan, 1999-2000
Kengo Kuma & Associates

This project is as much about the building as the landscape around it. Kengo Kuma is an architect who has expanded the role of architecture to encompass the area around his buildings. His attitude to site is interesting and varies in response to the particular project: at times, for example at the Kitakami Canal Museum, he has even buried his architecture. Kuma explains: 'Listening to the place is a method that has not been used by modern architects, but is, I think, something different. Personally I use this method in the belief that it is consistent.'

In the History Museum at Nasu he has produced a building with a classically Japanese response to site. Nasu is in the mountains of Tochigi Prefecture in northern Honshu, an area with many pine forests. The views from the Museum extend to an area of cleared coniferous forest, which for this writer has something of the feeling of the eighteenth-century forest park of Tsarskoye Selo in Saint Petersburg. The design of the building and surrounding grounds show a sublime appreciation of the northern forest clearing.

Kuma is also known for his wide use of materials: bamboo, stone, glass, paper and straw. In Nasu he has designed two museums. The Stone Museum is an almost blank, solid building of stone, not surprisingly. However, at Nasu History Museum the boundary between architecture and landscape is blurred through the use of glass and then re-established by the use of screens. The museum's design creates a special feeling of openness, the essence of traditional Japanese architecture. The translucent screens were made by attaching straw to aluminium mesh with resin; there are also other open panels made of local vines within a metal frame. Such a transparent design using natural materials evokes *Sukiya*, an attitude to building from the early Edo period in the seventeenth century. The minimalist

architecture composes and reveals the historical artefacts: a stone gateway, an old storehouse, and architectural features such as a column from a school.

From a landscape design point of view what is so seductive here is the exquisite simplicity of the external spaces. These consist of modulated bands of gravel under the eaves, simple orthogonal footpaths, and sprig-planted grassed lawns, which will eventually change from the current line pattern to a more even grass texture. Beyond the lawns are the lines of thin etiolated trunks of pine trees revealed after forest clearance. The spaces within and without the museum are bathed in light. The impact of such simplicity on the West could be seen to explain much of the ambition of the Modern Movement (the most obvious comparison is with such buildings as Mies van der Rohe's Farnsworth House), but then the viewer realizes that the Nasu Museum is profoundly non-Western and carries on a school of thought that appreciates materials whether traditional or new. The low-lying building, with its pitched roof and large overhangs, continues the *Sukiya* tradition. This is a project by an architect who appreciates site: 'Imagine fine particles floating over the earth. My aim is to create a similar condition. Let me be clear. My aim is not to create particle-like works of architecture. I want to create a condition that is as vague and ambiguous as drifting particles.'

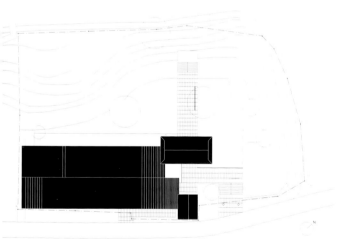

Above: Plan showing the relationship between the building and the surrounding landscape. The open grassed glades are to the east and west of the museum, with the forest beyond.

Right: View from the overhanging roof of the western façade showing the relationship between the architectural space and the landscape.

Top right: The entrance is a reinterpretation of the Japanese architectural tradition.

Above. The eastern façade with the approach road to the left. The glass façade appears to rise directly from the gravel.

Right: The feeling of being outside is continued inside the building.

Above: When the museum site was cleared of forest, the trees from the inner section were left exposed and were distinctively straight, thin and bare.

This appearance will change as they are exposed to wind and sun. The pattern formed by the grass is a result of sprig planting.

This page: The straw panels inside the building can be adjusted to compose different views of the forest outside.

Parc de la Théols
Issoudun, Indre, Val de Loire, France, 1992-95
Desvigne & Dalnoky

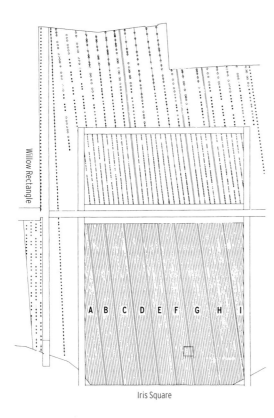

Willow Rectangle

A B C D E F G H I

Iris Square

Issoudun is a historic medieval town - once part of the old dukedom of Berry - on the banks of the River Théols, south-west of Bourges. Michel Desvigne of Desvigne & Dalnoky has created a 2.47 hectare (6 acre) town park on a floodable riverside area which was once used as allotments or vegetable gardens but which had become derelict. Desvigne won the competition for the commission in 1992 on the basis that his proposal reflected the history of the site and particularly the field boundaries. Desvigne has directly linked the routes through the park to spaces and landmarks in the town such as the Saint-Paterne bridge, the museum of the Saint-Roch Hospice and the town square.

The simplicity of the park owes something to the limited budget (615,000). Essentially Desvigne has created a large rectangular garden - the Iris Square (Carré d'Iris) - within the old plot boundary, alongside the river on the northern (town side) riverbank. The field is planted with strips of irises of different colours, heights and seasons, and framed by a wooden boardwalk. The strips are set at a diagonal orientation. Beyond the Iris Square on the town side is the Willow Rectangle (Rectangle de Saules). This consists of lines of sometimes single and sometimes mixed species of willow (Salix sp.). Both trees and shrubs are planted in parallel offset alignment and are grouped by height. The largest are Salix cinerea, followed by the medium-sized willows Salix rosmarinifolia and Salix viminalis. The two smaller, groundcover willows are Salix purpurea nana gracilis and Salix repens nitida. There are also lines of Salix gracilistyla planted as hedges. The use of so many willow varieties is a subtle and unusual approach. Willows in such numbers are not only cheap, but on a flood plain they are also extremely quick to grow. The straight boardwalks become paths which link the park with the town and with two new footbridges across the Théols to the opposite bank.

On the south bank, away from the town, the effects are more pastoral. Grassed fields are planted with alternate rows of cherry (Prunus sp.) and apple (Malus sp.). Flowery effects have been created using baby's breath (Gypsophyla sp.), Cosmos sp. and knapweed (Centaurea sp.), with hedges of box (Buxus sempervirens) and bay laurel (Laurus nobilis). Along the riverbank, which is planted with jonquils (Narcissus), bullrushes (Typha sp.) and flag iris (Iris pseudoacorus), there is another boardwalk which leads to a little dock.

Desvigne summarizes the design thus: 'We had to transform these private allotments - without losing their original spirit - by creating a new dimension.' On plan this design appears to have an unnatural and almost obsessive rigour, but as a finished project it appears to be a very successful example of translating private gardening plots into an integrated public park form. This is an extremely economical exercise in creating spaces and making connections in a way which merges the pastoral to the bucolic.

Planting diagram of the Willow Rectangle (top) and the Iris Square (bottom). In the Rectangle the willows are arranged by height: from tall (Salix cinerea) at the top of the diagram, medium (Salix rosmarinfolia, Salix viminalis) and low (Salix purpurea nana gracilis), down to hedge (Salix gracilistyla) at the bottom of the Rectangle where it meets the Iris Square. In the Iris Square the iris are arranged as follows:
A medium blue, May-June, 90cm high
B yellow, April-May, 45-50cm high
C black, May-June, 95cm high
D pure white, May-June, 95cm high
E white, June-August, 50-60cm high
F blue, April-May, 50cm high
G clear yellow, May-June, 85-90cm high
H violet-blue, June-August, 100-110cm high
I yellow, May-June, 85-95cm high

Top right: View across the Iris Square towards the medieval town with the willows in the distance.

Right: The boardwalk of the Willow Rectangle with the yellow and blue of the Iris Square beyond.

Left: Site plan. The park
extends along the River
Théols and connects both
sides of the river with the
centre of town to the north.

Above: The boardwalk
alongside the Willow
Rectangle, with grey willow
(*Salix cinerea*) trees to
the left and osier (*Salix
viminalis*) shrubs to the right.

The Willow Rectangle is
composed of different shrub
willows with taller rows of
willow trees beyond.

The southern bank of the River Théols is planted with rows of cherry (*Prunus* sp.) and apple (*Malus* sp.) and grass fields. One of the two simple steel footbridges can be seen on the far left of the picture, with the dock on the right. This project is all about achieving strong and effective design on a minimum budget.

Whiteinch Cross
Glasgow, Scotland, UK, 1999
Gross Max

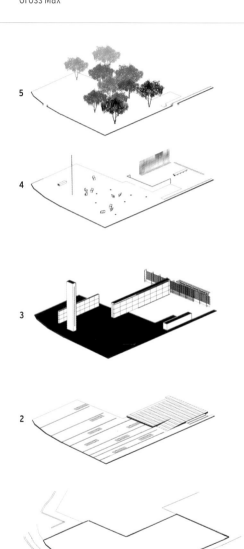

Two free-standing walls clad in Cor-ten steel, and a galvanized steel frame planted with wisteria climbers (*Wisteria sinensis*), are arranged as a 'T' in plan. These elements work together to define the spaces of a corner plot on Dumbarton Road, just north of the Clyde Tunnel in the West End of Glasgow. An 8 metre (26 foot) long sheet of water washes down the corner end of the Cor-ten wall, providing 'white noise' to counter the din of passing traffic. Standing guard is a tower by English light artist Adam Barker-Mill. At night, lit by a blue-filtered vertical light, it acts as a striking landmark. Also at night a grid of landing lights patterns the ground, while up-lighting picks out the steel frame and the water wall is backlit. The blue light of the tower and the lilac colour of the wisteria contrast with the orange to brown hues of the rusting Cor-ten steel – a material that acknowledges Glasgow's industrial heritage of steel-making and shipbuilding.

The square has two levels. In the lower part existing trees have been retained; these are protected by custom-built 1.2 x 4 metre (4 x 13 foot) cast-iron grilles. Seats made from black reinforced concrete have been placed at this level. The upper level is paved with large slabs of Clashach sandstone from the Moray Firth. Clashach quarry, near Elgin, reopened in 1986 and produces a honey-coloured sandstone with bands of ferrous markings – a feature that reinforces the tribute to Glasgow's heavy industry.

The £300,000 project was one of the schemes that made up the '5 Spaces Project', part of the programme for Glasgow's year as UK City of Design in 1999. The idea was that community-based housing associations would choose key sites and then work with artists and landscape designers to create open spaces and squares that would transform awkward corners of the city.

Gross Max comprises Eelco Hooftman (who comes from The Netherlands) and Briton Bridget Baines, both of whom teach at the School of Landscape, Edinburgh College of Art. After this project they have gone on to work on a series of urban square projects in London, to be implemented in locations as diverse as Hammersmith and Hackney. Integral to their design is their use of 'layering'. Hooftman talks of the 'sensuous striptease unravelling the layers of the landscape'; he sees the city as both an organic and an artificial landscape, layered with history. At Whiteinch Cross the layering is directly expressed, creating a space that is impressive in its simplicity.

Above: Axonometric drawings illustrating the layers of the site:
1. vacant city corner plot
2. the ground layer of two levels
3. the vertical elements of walls, frame and tower
4. the confetti-like scatter of seats and water walls
5. tree vegetation layer

Above: View of the site's name marker, and behind it the Cor-ten steel-covered wall with its sheet of falling water. On the right is the galvanized steel climber-plant frame.

Above: A pavement of Clashach sandstone slabs is ████████ ████████ seats, while trees grow out of cast-iron grilles. The wall of rusting Cor-ten steel – a material first developed for North American railroad freight cars in the 1930s – provides a strong, bright backdrop.

Right: At night a grid of landing lights patterns the ███████ ███ ██ ██ █████ frame and backlit water wall contrast with the vertical blue light of Adam Barker-Mill's tower.

Above: The simple,
geometric lines of the
galvanized climbing plant
frame where it meets the
end of the Cor-ten wall
demonstrate Gross Max's
pared-down approach.

Above: The zigzag seats, in polished black pre-cast concrete, display a minimalism beyond modernism. They could almost be by Philippe Starck.

Enschede Station
Enschede, The Netherlands, 1994–2001
OKRA

Railway stations are major transport interchanges and arrival points in The Netherlands. Important as town gateways, they tend to be seen by municipalities as a kind of 'architectural calling card'. The Enschede Station project has an additional dimension, however. Although Enschede is at the eastern edge of The Netherlands, the opening up of borders within the European Union means that it is no longer at the periphery of economic activity. The station development is part of an urban revitalization programme that aims to create a new and vibrant business area. Public spaces are here seen as an important spur to urban redevelopment.

The development around Enschede Station extends over 13 hectares (32 acres), largely on the south or town centre side of the station. The station itself is primarily a terminus, with one through line on the north side. A main aim of the development was to improve connections between the railway station and town centre. South of the tracks there are three main public spaces: the bus station (the Busplein), to the west; a major new town square, the Bomenplein (Tree Square), in front of the station, leading due south to the old town centre; and a long station forecourt (the Voorplein), which runs parallel with the railway. North of the tracks is a new garden area, the Stationstuin. The combined cost of the public spaces was 23 million euros. Work began in 1994, with the bus station and Bomenplein being completed first (in 1997).

The open spaces have been designed to celebrate arrival to the town. The Bomenplein is an urban gateway and a place to meet; it is designed as a 1:1.4 rectangle, demarcated by a square grid of in situ concrete edged with steel and marked by uplighters. On the south side of the square are 20 honey locust trees (*Gleditsia triacanthos*) alternating with stele-like light columns. Seating is by way of bench seats, each composed of a vertical concrete structure encased in curved timber which cantilevers to form a seat. The Busplein is an exercise in simple functionalism: the asphalt pavement is patterned with a confetti-like sprinkling of light stone insets, while the low concrete platforms and bus stands are marked by an identical confetti pattern of dark stone on the lighter concrete. On the railway station side of the Busplein can be seen the sweep of a long curved balustrade, with lines of bicycles beyond, while along the Bomenplein side is a steel canopy by I/AA Architects.

The long Voorplein is situated to the east of the Bomenplein, and is the most recently completed part of the development. It plays with the slope of the land, which falls across the site from east to west. Across the square a long mirror pool appears to rise from the sloping paving. Two lines of trees demarcate respectively the north and south sides of this area, opening out to the station and the Bomenplein. To the north of the station, meanwhile, the garden area provides a new green entry point. OKRA's no-nonsense, functional approach has produced a versatile, welcoming series of spaces that are equally effective both day and night.

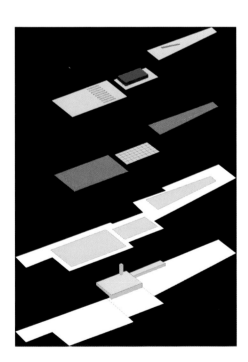

Above: The 'layers' of the public spaces south of the station. From bottom: the three main areas (yellow), and the station (grey); the three squares, or *pleinen* (grey); the surfaces, gridded in the centre and monolithic to left and right; and the top layer, featuring trees (green, centre) and the mirror pool (diagonal, right).

Left: Acting like a spirit level, the mirror pool emphasizes the incline of the Voorplein as it slopes away beneath.

Above: The *Bomenplein* in front of the station building, looking west to the bus station. A simple canopy shelter separates the two spaces. The concrete paving is a simple and subtly modulated grid.

Top right: Evening view of
the station front as seen
from the mirror pool across
the voorplein, with the
station to the right.

Right: Plan showing the
three spaces round the
railway (with the bus station
to the left). These spaces
are all paved, whereas north
of the tracks the garden
area is much greener.

With its metal-edged concrete grid set off by the verticals of trees and light columns, the Bomenplein is the station entrance square and an exercise in controlled geometry. The timber benches provide a warm note. At night, and in the rain, this space becomes very much alive.

Left: The north side of the complex abuts the railway station and this juxtaposition has been emphasized by a curved platform and underlit benches.

Above: North of the station is a garden area with simple bound gravel paving and a green lawn. The steps and walls are in simple, fair-faced concrete. This project is characterized by simple, economic and effective construction.

Matchworks
Liverpool, UK, 1998–2002
Brodie McAllister and shedkm

The old Bryant and May match factory, built in 1918 by the River Mersey at Garston in south Liverpool, is a ferroconcrete building with metal windows and large areas of glazing. As a classic early twentieth-century industrial building it is now considered a place of historic interest. The factory has been refurbished as business units by the Liverpool-based architects shedkm and the whole site has become a 'business village' developed by the Speke Garston Development Company.

The landscape design reflects the site's industrial past – materials include rubber, glass, steel and concrete and are used in honest and simple ways. Raised planters of grey painted steel (made by a local shipbuilder) are used to separate parking bays as are gabion-walled planters filled with dark granite. The use of granite corresponds to the original industrial tramway – paved with grey granite setts – which once connected the factory to the wharves on the Mersey. The gabion planters are mass-planted with rock rose shrubs (*Helianthemum sp.*) to mirror the flower motif on the front of the original building. The parking area is paved in macadam with rivet-like domed steel studs and seating is made from blackened sewer pipes fixed by metal stands.

Parking has been organized orthogonally north and south of the building and the complex is approached by an avenue of white poplar trees (*Populus alba*) set out symmetrically on the central axis of the façade. The use of poplar refers to the building's original function – the matches were made of poplar and the timber was stored nearby. At night the avenue is emphasized by uplighters and the façade of the main building is lit and reflected in the blacktop.

There is a meadow at the front of the Matchworks and McAllister talks of burning it annually once it has grown (a traditional way of managing long grass but one that is unlikely to happen in a city business park due to smoke control rules). The idea behind the long grass is to hide the view of the parking area from the approach road and to allow the building to 'float' in a prairie, recalling the American plains. On the site's periphery there is a zone of scrubland, which will be allowed to develop naturally into woodland.

This is a scheme that uses the standard elements of the business park but has rejuvenated them by expressing the history of the site. The development has taken Liverpool's industrial inheritance and transformed it into jobs and economic revitalization.

Above: At night the development takes on a drama and the symmetry of the façade focuses on the water tower. Uplighters guide the way through the avenue of white poplar (*Populus alba*).

Top: When seen from the approach road the front of the building seems to float in a prairie of long grass.

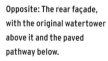

Opposite: The rear façade, with the original watertower above it and the paved pathway below.

Opposite: Gabion-walled planters and red pre-cast concrete slabs are simplicity itself and do not fight with the monumental façade or the new silver-clad steel service cores.

Above: In this image the hard paving continues under the bridge, creating a visual link across the threshold to the logfield beyond, where logs were once stored to make the matchsticks.

Right: Plan showing the main building at the centre with the steel planters at right angles to the front (bottom of plan) and the gabion planters to the rear. The black area at the top represents light-industrial units. The meadow is bottom left and the logfield top right.

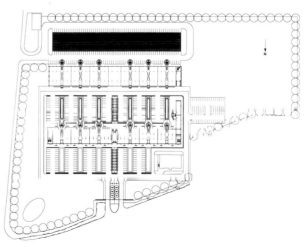

chapter 3 post-industrial

The latter half of the twentieth century saw an aesthetic shift equivalent to the Romantic movement at the end of the eighteenth century. The Romantics appreciated the sublime scenery of the Alps and England's Lake District while previously these had been seen as horrid and dangerous places. The comparably sublime landscapes of industry can be appreciated for their intrinsic qualities as well as for what they represent in terms of cultural and social history for the towns and people that survive around them. This reappraisal began with the study of industrial archaeology in the 1960s and the foundation in England of industrial museums such as Ironbridge in Shropshire (from 1967) and Beamish in County Durham (conceived in 1958 and opened in 1971).

Some would cite Richard Haag's Gasworks Park in Seattle (1975) as the prototypical post-industrial landscape design', but Gasworks Park is very much an industrial object placed in a grass field. In the 1980s and 1990s Peter and Anneliese Latz's Hafeninsel Bürgerpark in Saarbrücken and Duisburg Nord Landsape Park - and indeed many of the other Emscher Park Internationale Bauaustellung projects - aimed at placing a wider value on the industrial inheritance of the landscape.

The Emscher Park IBA (1989-99) involved the open space development and greening of the coal mines and steelworks of the Ruhr Basin, but not the destruction of the evidence of those steelworks or of the mine workings and pit heaps. These pit heaps are monuments to nineteenth- and twentieth-century coalmining and were made on a geological scale. They are the landmarks of the Ruhr area. Contrast this approach with Durham County Council's policy in the 1960s of removing or remodelling the pit heaps visible from the Great North Road in order to lose the evidence of the industrial history of the area: to make it something else. In the 1960s Durham wished to abolish the signs of its coalmining history, and indeed that was also the policy in Germany at the time. By the 1990s, however, the aim in North Rhine-Westphalia was to conserve and appreciate the industrial heritage, including pit heaps, steelworks and indeed the tallest gasometer in Europe.

Post-industrial landscape design is characterized by the retention of industrial artefacts, as at Völklingen Ironworks (pages 82-83) and Ferropolis (pages 84-87); by opening up to the public areas that were previously closed; by the encouragement of ruderal vegetation (allowing natural regeneration to occur spontaneously and only modifying that by management); by the need to render safe toxic and contaminated land and finally, but fundamentally, by an aesthetic, social and historical appreciation of industry. It may also be associated with an appreciation of the palimpsests of historical layers that form most landscapes: one human activity and its markings superimposed upon another. This is indeed the main design thrust of Bernard Huet's Parc de Bercy (1995) in the old wine market in Paris, where each historical layer is given expression on the ground with overlapping and deliberately counterpoised grids.

The Negev Phosphate Mine at Zin in Israel (pages 98-101) is in a different order from Völkingen or Ferropolis. Rather it is an exercise in working with an extractive industry and modifying the results. The spoil can hardly be hidden away or disguised, so it is formed in a way that works with the original geomorphology of the Zin Valley and in a way that is intended to reduce its impact. The forms themselves are sublime, but set within a greater and more sublime landscape.

At Hedeland in Denmark (pages 88-91) the extractive industry forms a changing backdrop to the stage, and like the Negev Project, the gravel workings are still operational. As at Ferropolis (and also at Duisburg Nord) such landscapes are seen as suitable backdrops for dramatic performances in a way comparable to the continuing use of Ancient Greek and Roman theatres and arenas in Europe.

At Dionyssos Quarries (pages 92-97) the post-industrial approach has become a form of land art, using the techniques of quarrying to remodel, save, view and reveal the historical quarries, while at Südgelände in Berlin (pages 102-105) ruderal vegetation has been allowed to progress for more than forty years thanks to the political division of Berlin. Without this unintentional political protection an area right in the middle of Berlin would never have been left to develop into birch woodland. Now site management as well as landscape design is further protecting this natural process of vegetation development.

Endnotes
1 for example Alan Tate:
Great City Parks (London,
Spon Press, 2001, p.114)

Völklingen Ironworks
Völklingen, Saarland, Germany, 1995-
Latz + Partner

Völklingen is in part a story of industrial history, but is also a story of dealing with the toxic results of that heritage, of land contaminated with hydrocarbons that have penetrated and poisoned the ground. The Völklingen Ironworks was established in 1873 and was taken over and expanded in 1881 by the Röchling brothers. The works grew to be a large plant for the production of pig iron. There are six blast furnaces and 18 hot blast stoves of which the oldest dates from 1885. The tower structure for the furnaces dates from 1916, but a substantial part of the original coking plant survives, including structures dating back to the 1890s - indeed the Old Coking Tower (Alte Koheturm) is the oldest in Germany. Overall this is a well-preserved ironworks where all parts of the process of pig iron production can still be seen. The water tanks are prominent in the town's skyline and rise to over 40 metres (130 feet), while the blast furnaces rise to 36 metres (118 feet). The ironworks closed in 1986 and in 1994 it was declared a UNESCO World Heritage site.

Peter and Anneliese Latz of Latz + Partner are known for their work on former industrial sites such as at the Hafeninsel Bürgerpark (1985-9) in Saarbrücken and Duisburg Nord Landscape Park (1990-2001). In 1995 Latz + Partner won the first prize in the competition for the conservation of the former coal tar and benzole plant, and are now developing the masterplan for the whole site. Their 1995 competition proposal was to construct a 2 hectare (5 acre) public park in the form of an earth sculpture on top of encapsulated toxic waste. Contaminated material from the plant was to be collected and buried and then sealed so rainwater could not wash out the toxic pollutants. The park itself was planned as a grove with flowering trees, secret gardens and clear water ponds, the surface water being channelled to a rivulet that surrounds the sealed Pollution Hill.

Latz + Partner worked on the competition with the Luxembourg architect Christian Bauer, who developed the service buildings on the edge of the park. In 1996 they were commissioned to carry out further developments by the owners, the Saarmontan Company. Unfortunately due to political reasons and changing ownership the 1995 plan was not carried out and indeed may never be.

In 2001 the present-day owner, the European Centre for Art and Industrial Culture UNESCO World Cultural Heritage Völklingen Works commissioned Latz + Partner to develop the masterplan for a wider 18 hectare (44 acre) site. The masterplan includes the 6 hectare (15 acre) World Cultural Heritage blast furnace site as well as 12 hectares (30 acres) of the surrounding former industrial area. The goal is to develop a concept that befits a world heritage site and that allows large numbers of people to visit the historic industrial monuments and to enjoy special events. The project also aims to develop a public riverside landscape

open to the inhabitants of the Völklingen area, including the possibility for providing leisure and refreshment facilities.

There are currently several design developments underway, including the provision of a safe network of passable tracks, paths and footbridges in areas that are not presently accessible as part of an overall circulation strategy. The vegetation concept allows for the carefully directed development and maintenance of spontaneously growing vegetation while retaining important vistas. Plans for water management include developing the existing drainage systems, while sealed areas and basins will be used to integrate 'water' as a landscape element on the site (as at the Duisburg Nord Landscape Park). In addition to this, the toxic pollutant treatment policy is still being developed.

In spite of the enormous task to hand, this form of landscape architecture is as much about knowing what to leave alone. It is in part an exercise in cultural appreciation as well as conservation. Sometimes a project is more a question of conserving what is already there than of radical change. Ruderal vegetation is allowed to flourish and natural processes are not impeded. Interventions are as much concerned with public health and safety as they are with design. The results are exercises in the sublime and an appreciation of industrial history.

Above: Industrial structures like this were once off limits to the majority of the population, but now members of the public will be able to visit and understand something of the dangerous world inhabited by the the 17,000 people who worked at the ironworks at its peak in 1957.

Right: Like the Ruhr Basin, the Saarland contains impressive industrial landscapes.

Top right: The ironworks' structures dominate the skyline of Völklingen.

Ruderal vegetation is now
growing in the once infertile
ground, and this will be
managed as part of the
landscape proposals.

Above: The coarse gravelled
parking area with two toilet
blocks left and right, ticket
blocks on the far side and
the slopes of the ski
mountain to left. This is
a simple scheme with
appropriately rough details
– not a place to visit in
high heels.

Left: The Hedeland 'foundation stone' has the appearance of a prehistoric monolith.

Top: The simple turf roofed ticket office. Boulders are used as a markers.

Above: One of the toilet blocks with its turf roof and walls

Dionyssos Quarries
Mount Pendelikón, Attica, Greece, 1994-7
Nella Golanda and Aspassia Kouzoupi

Mount Pendelikón was the source of the marble used to build the Parthenon. With such a long and distinguished history – dating back to the early fifth century BC – the marble quarries deserved to be celebrated. Thus was born the idea of an open air museum, which would allow the workings to be viewed safely and to be explained. The landscape sculptor Nella Golanda and architect Aspassia Kouzoupi worked on the museum from 1994 to 1997. They were assisted by five quarry workers who had been employed at the site until its closure around 1970. The quarry has a total area of 3,500 square metres (38,000 square feet). While in use it had been worked using traditional techniques, which exploited the natural lines of the rock strata. These had been wedged, hammered and cracked open with the aid of water; as a result the rock faces had become a sculptural composition, revealing even more clearly the lines of the rock. Golanda and Kouzoupi wished to reveal the workings and rock faces.

The museum essentially consists of a series of paths through the old quarry. In its construction Golanda and Kouzoupi used marble from the piles of stone found at the foot of each hollowed-out rock face; these were cut using traditional techniques. Parts of the quarry face had been buried by rubble, which was removed to show the rock face. No mortar, concrete or other imported building materials were used in the museum; indeed, the quarry is inaccessible to machinery.

The museum is set beside a ramped slide that survives from the original quarry. Traditionally, stone was worked on in the quarry and then slid down the hillside on a prepared ramp – a method used by the Ancient Egyptians. And of course the ramp has been preserved. Approaching the museum, the visitor first encounters a small entrance square at the foot of the quarry. Around the square a series of enclosures, protected by low retaining walls, has been built; these protect visitors from steep slopes of loose rocks which were too dangerous to be reworked. Also near the entrance is a building that houses services for the museum.

A network of paths leads up the hillside through the quarry area. These are mostly the original quarry paths waymarked or emphasized, and made safe. A number of features from the original quarry still survive – such as the method of holding the blocks of stone onto the ramped slide – and these are carefully revealed. The site is not merely of historical interest, however; the designers also wanted it to contain surprise elements, and the climb ends in a hollowed belvedere with stunning views towards the sea. Using traditional industrial techniques Golanda and Kouzoupi have created a truly post-industrial landscape of sublime grandeur.

Left: Drawing showing a reworked face, with the pile of rock waste below.

Top: The quarry has a number of different faces, each with its own pile of discarded stones and waste material.

Opposite: Steps lead into the heart of the quarry. Like all structures in the museum, these were built by hand using dry stone walling techniques.

Overleaf: The main route through the open air museum. The geological landscape, worked over thousands of years, possesses a stark grandeur.

Left: The belvedere affords spectacular views over the Attica countryside and towards the Aegean Sea.

Top left and above: Early sketches for the museum.

Top right: Paths of varied widths meander through the sculptural forms of the quarry waste.

Above: The services
building, situated at the
ѕⅼѳⱤₑ ѳₓ ₜⱨₑ ₚₐₜⱨ ₜⱨₑₒᵤₘⱨ
the quarry, was constructed
ᵂⁱₜⱨₒᵤₜ ₜⱨₑ ᵤₛₑ ₒₓ ₘₒᵣₜₐᵣ.
A retaining wall protects
against loose quarry
material.

Negev Phosphate Works
Zin, Negev Desert, Israel, 1990-
Shlomo Aronson

The northern Negev desert of Israel has been extensively opencast mined for phosphate, leaving large holes and square mountains of spoil. The fill material was dumped to create steep slopes - geometrical 'engineered' forms of up to 40 metres (130 feet) in height. The vast scale of the tipped material was, however, entirely foreign to the landscape of the Zin Valley. This is an impressive desert wadi landscape of crescent-shaped hogback hills which is also subject to flash floods.

In 1990, following pressure from the Nature Reserve Authority (now the Israeli Nature and National Parks Protection Authority), the Negev Phosphates Company, which became part of Rotem Amfert Negev and ICL, commissioned Israeli landscape architect Shlomo Aronson to design a more environmentally sensitive approach to opencast phosphate mining. Aronson wished to work with the existing landscape and devised methods of filling in the excavations left by mining with spoil material.

The Zin mine covers 265 hectares (655 acres) of the 120 km (620 mile) long Zin Valley, south-east of Beersheva. The phosphate exists in differing grades and is buried under some 16 metres (52 feet) of alluvial material and 8 metres (26 feet) of clay. Sometimes there are two layers of phosphate separated by other material. The phosphate is used for fertilizer and is shipped by railway northwards.

Aronson's solution to the problems of the landsape has four main elements. First, the conservation of the wadi - which runs through the centre of the site - breaks the mounds of spoil in two and immediately reduces the scale of their visual impact, while also conserving the side slopes of the Zin Valley. Second, the extent of the works has been contained and restricted, with all earth moving confined to the mine itself. The result is a sort of logistical musical chairs in which material had to be moved to already excavated areas. The challenge lay in the fact that the design had to work within the constraints of the different grades of phosphate-bearing rock and the limitation of working with 100-tonne trucks. Third, new landforms are based on a crescent-shaped plan and given hogback shapes to reflect the existing topography. Fourth, the impact of the height and hence the scale of the earthworks was reduced by creating 10 metre (33 foot) high setbacks instead of the 30 to 40 metre (100 to 130 foot) straight-sided mounds of the earlier mines.

Work began in 1990 and in phase one some 3 million cubic metres (11 million cubic feet) of overburden was removed to reach the underlying phosphate layers and 40 million cubic metres (156 million cubic feet) of material shifted. It is anticipated that mining will continue for just over a decade. In total 100 million cubic metres (390 million cubic feet) of material is being reshaped to create the large sculptural forms that mirror the shapes of the surrounding mountains.

This is a form of industrial land art where the landscape architect acts as a sculptor, recreating landforms that are in sympathy with the existing desert topography.

Top right: A photograph from 1996 showing the new landscape forms within the Zin Valley context.

Right: Model showing the final earth forms.

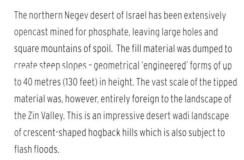
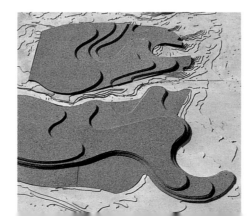

Photograph taken in 1991 at the beginning of the project. Paths left by the haulage routes used to remove the 3 million tonnes of overburden are clearly visible, while the top crescent shaped terrace is still under construction.

Previously the spoil heaps had straight-sided 40 metre (120 foot) drops. The newly terraced spoil heaps, with their shorter, sloping drops, are shown here with the landscape of the hogback hills beyond. This photograph illustrates the impact that the terraces have on the surrounding landscape.

Südgelände Nature Park
Berlin, Germany, 1996-2000
ÖkoCon and planland

Berlin has re-invented itself since re-unification, but it still bears many traces of its post-1945 divisions. The Schöneberger Südgelände were built between 1880 and 1890 as freight marshalling yards to serve Tempelhof station, but they lay derelict after closing in 1952. The yards originally extended to 70 hectares (173 acres) in the heart of Berlin, and of this some 25 hectares (62 acres) in total has been conserved. The site lies just south of the old Anhalter Bahnhof along the line of the Berlin Wall, between Tempelhof and Schöneberg. Before re-unification the division of the city and the division of responsibility for the railways - the East German Reichsbahn operated railways in the western part of the city - created administrative and legal problems, making this area a no man's land. The isolation was also a form of protection, however, and from dereliction grew the natural regeneration of birch woods and groves of poplars and *Robinia*. A form of nature was growing out of the railway lines, colonizing the cuttings and embankments, viaducts and ramps which formed the yards. The result is a mosaic of habitat types - dry and open, shaded and damp - which by 1991 was 70 per cent woodland. The coarse, well-drained old railway ballast gives rise to vivid spring vegetation effects.

Though little needed to be done, the designers' main aims were to protect the area from development, to manage the vegetation and to provide access for the general public. It has also been necessary to conserve the remains and artefacts of the railway days, ranging from the water tower to turntables and old locomotives.

The major design gesture is a central walkway raised 800mm (32 inches) above the vegetation to give access across the 4 hectare (10 acre) nature conservation area, which is otherwise closed to public access. This straight walkway - a simple steel grille with edge supports - is about 600 metres (1,970 feet) long and runs over the railway tracks. Indeed, the railway lines act as the foundation for the walkway. The public are not allowed to leave the walkway. Its designers, the art group Odious, are now based in the old engine shed.

Although the public are not allowed to leave the walkway in that part of the park, elsewhere public access is unrestricted and the footpaths are composed of old railway ballast. Vegetation management has consisted of mowing clearings as well as removing some trees and tree roots, so that in some areas natural succession has been halted. The result is a series of glades in the woodland. The aim is to open up this *terra incognita* to the inhabitants of the city so that they can enjoy the fruits of 45 years of neglect and isolation.

**Above: Tempelhof
marshalling yards in 1930.**

**Top: The main entrance
approach is a grass ramp
with the railway viaduct
beyond.**

Above: This old turntable has been restored – the industrial heritage is remembered.

Right: The 1995 overall plan.

NATUR-PARK SÜDGELÄNDE
Entwurf

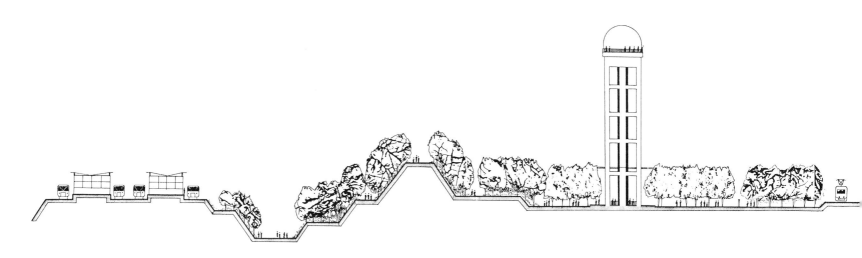

Opposite: The site is a place
of controlled dereliction –
the water tower has been
restored, birch woods grow
from the railway tracks and
a steam locomotive (a
2-10-0 Kriegslok freight
engine) lies unrestored.

Top: Metal walkways with
Cor-ten steel pillars give
access across the 4
hectare (9 acre) nature
conservation area.

Above: This section between
Priesterweg station on the
left and the Water Tower
gives an idea of the
variations of habitat type
provided by the exposed
embankments and shaded
cuttings of the designs.

places of allegory and meaning

The idea of the allegorical garden - whether in the English picturesque or the French formal style - is characteristic of the eighteenth century. The usual point of reference was classical myth, for example The Elysian Fields at Stowe, England, though national mythologies were also represented - Stowe also boasts William Kent's Temple of British Worthies. It was a conceit that formed the basis of landscape gardening in England until the arrival of Lancelot Brown in the 1780s. Such landscapes of meaning can prompt political reactions. In the late twentieth century Ian Hamilton-Finlay was banned by the French government from contributing to their 1989 bicentenary exhibitions because of his interest in and wish to represent the garden of Hitler's minister, Albert Speer, created during his imprisonment in Spandau.

Allegory is something that the proponents of the Modern Movement often wished to remove in their desire for pure functional form. That is not to say that the allegorical garden died with the advent of Modernism. The greatest twentieth-century English exponent of allegorical landscape design is Sir Geoffrey Jellicoe. At the Runnymede John F. Kennedy Memorial Garden (1964) Jellicoe took as his inspiration John Bunyan's poem *The Pilgrim's Progress* and Giovanni Bellini's painting *Allegory of the Progress of the Soul*. This commission eventually led to his work on the Sutton Place Garden in the 1980s, which deals with the ideas of Creation, Life and Aspiration.

Such ideas and conceits have enjoyed a renewed interest among landscape designers over the past 20 years, and are central to the work of Robert Camlin (pages 118-121) or Christophe Girot (pages 122-125). By contrast El Cedazo in Aguascalientes, Mexico by Grupo de Diseño Urbano (pages 108-113) is partly about giving a new meaning to a seventeenth-century reservoir and partly about expressing the function of a recreation park using the vocabulary of contemporary life in a modern industrial city: steel buildings and concrete.

The Jewish Museum in Berlin (pages 114-117) is much more overtly allegorical, since its prime function is one of remembrance. Traces of old Berlin, such as the paving of Hollmannstrasse, have been retained; a tribute to the Jewish poet Paul Celan has been created with paving based on drawings by Celan's wife, and ideas of nature are represented in the Paradise Garden. The result is an elegy.

At MeSci in Tokyo (pages 126-129) George Hargreaves has created a new landscape on a recently reclaimed site. The gardens each represent a scientific theme. Green pyramids emerge from the informal lake to express the colliding and fusing of molecules; undulating landforms and wave walls represent the light, sound and electronic waves and in the central promenade, rolling landforms with randomly placed wind sculptures represent the winds of Tokyo Bay.

The concept behind Insel Hombroich (pages 130-137) was to create an ideal alternative world set within an ideal landscape of woods, marsh and wetland with elements of old gardens. The site is also inhabited by both open-air artworks and a series of pavilions to house art collections. This is a twentieth-century exercise in taste on an eighteenth-century scale. It is a place of retreat.

By contrast, the two Australian schemes in this chapter are about contemporary life. The Northam Mulark Community project in Western Australia (pages 138-141) seeks to create an identity and recognition for a dispossessed people, allowing them to present their view of what the land means to them. In the Garden of Australian Dreams in Canberra (pages 142-147) Richard Weller and Vladimir Sitta have given a physical form to ideas of what Australia means and in doing so have composed new landscape forms.

El Cedazo Park

Aguascalientes, Mexico, 1995
Grupo de Diseño Urbano

Aguascalientes, which takes its name from the thermal springs on which it is built, is north of Guadalajara in central Mexico and sits 1,800 metres (5,900 feet) above sea level on the high plateau of the Sierra Madre Occidental, with a fairly low rainfall of 500mm (20 inches) a year. It is a growing industrial city with a population of 650,000, a Nissan car plant and all the problems of a developing community, including the construction of low-cost housing with inadequate social services and the despoliation of the landscape by development. Grupo de Diseño Urbano (GDU) have designed two parks in Aguascalientes that centre on existing *presas* or reservoirs. Parque Mexico (1995) is based on a nineteenth-century reservoir built to power a textile mill. El Cedazo was built as a drinking water reservoir in 1525 (hence the name: *cedazo* means sieve and refers to the reservoir filter layers). There is also a surviving 4 kilometre (2½ mile) long subterranean aqueduct to carry the water to the old city. By the 1990s the water was crossed by high-voltage power lines and surrounded by low-income housing. Meanwhile the reservoir had silted up, the earth dam had started to leak and the place had become generally unsavoury. It was a place for drug dealing and despair, where the walls bore graffiti such as '*No vale la pena de vivir*' ('life's not worth living').

The area has been transformed into a 64 hectare (160 acre) state park with an appropriate maintenance staff and parks police on bicycles. Mario Schjetnan, head of GDU, says, 'This park is about two things, social issues and the restoration of an old environmental feature of the city (i.e. the reservoir).' Schjetnan studied architecture in Mexico and then landscape architecture at Berkeley. He is also a disciple and friend of the late Luís Barragán. Like Barragán, Schjetnan's work is characterized by the use of water and strong, local colour washes.

The park lies on both sides of the reservoir and is entered from the Boulevard Aguascalientes Ote to the east. By the entrance is the Cultural Centre (also designed by GDU) – a series of workshops arranged around two plazas – where there are classes for young people in art, music and dance. To the west, alongside the lake edge, there is a cafeteria with a waterfront terrace. From the terrace it is possible to cross the lake via a walkway which has a mesh underneath to trap floating debris. Around the lake there are paths of crushed volcanic stone providing routes for both pedestrians and cyclists. The development also includes a range of sports fields and courts for basketball, volleyball and soccer, as well as indoor gymnasia.

At the western end of the park is the now repaired and replanted dam, from which there are views westwards to the mountains of the Sierra Madre. Next to the dam there is an amphitheatre with views to the north-east of the lake. There are also a number of children's playgrounds and the park links with an ecological zone to the west downstream of the dam. Vegetation consists of old, preserved pepper (*Schinus molle*) and huizache (*Acacia farnesiana*) trees and newly planted Italian cypress (*Cupressus sempervirens*). In order to protect it from vandalism the new park is enclosed by a fence of brightly painted 1.8 metre (6 foot) high steel rods. There is a three peso entrance fee for adults (one peso for children) and the park is closed at night and on Mondays for maintenance.

In his 1998 *Landscape Architecture* article Bill Thompson concludes: 'El Cedazo is not a narrative landscape that attempts to re-create history and myth, rather, it celebrates the industrial future of Aguascalientes with its contemporary use of heavy duty built elements, some of them manufactured locally.' As a child's painting in the Cutural Centre was labelled: '*Alegría y diversión - mis vacaciones en El Cedazo*' ('Happiness and fun - my holidays in El Cedazo'). This is a park providing happiness and fun in a neighbourhood that once knew only despair.

Top right: The cafeteria and terrace seen from across the lake.

Right: The Rose Walk, which crosses the dam, is covered by a metal structure to provide shade.

Above: One of the Cultural Centre's two plazas with workshops to the left and (to the right) a landmark tower vibrantly coloured in the GDU colouring – in the Barragán tradition.

Top: Shaded picnic area.

Above: The cafeteria and *mirador* (lookout point) seen from the walkway spanning the lake. Meshes under the walkway act as a trap for debris.

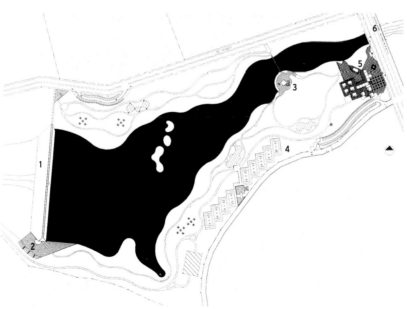

Top: Lakeside terrace.

Plan of the park.
1. Dam
2. Amphitheatre
3. Cafeteria
4. Sports grounds
5. Cultural Centre
6. Boulevard Aguascalientes

Overleaf: Stepped paving
leads to the lakeside, with
the dam on the right.

Jewish Museum
Kreuzberg, Berlin, Germany, 1990-99
Cornelia Müller and Jan Wehberg (MKW)

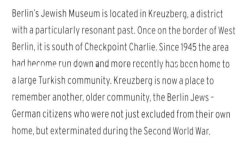

Berlin's Jewish Museum is located in Kreuzberg, a district with a particularly resonant past. Once on the border of West Berlin, it is south of Checkpoint Charlie. Since 1945 the area had become run down and more recently has been home to a large Turkish community. Kreuzberg is now a place to remember another, older community, the Berlin Jews – German citizens who were not just excluded from their own home, but exterminated during the Second World War.

The history of the museum is also interesting. Originally it was planned as a new department within the Berlin City Museum on Lindenstrasse, then housed in the Prussian-built Collegienhaus. The extension was to be the home of the Berlin Museum's Jewish collection, but after much discussion the project grew from a Jewish Department within the Berlin Museum to a fully-fledged national museum of Jewish life in Germany, covering 2,000 years of history. Now the Collegienhaus has become the entrance to the Jewish Museum. Once it had been completed in 1998 the public were allowed into Daniel Libeskind's empty building for two years before the permanent exhibition was finally installed and opened in September 2001. In these two years 350,000 people viewed the empty building.

References to the history of Berlin's Jews are implicit in the site's design – references which can be found, for example, in the composition of the paving, or the lines on the building, in the engraved stones and in the use of gravel to emphasize the 'voids' created by the forms of the building.

To the south is the concrete-walled ETA Hoffmann Garden of Exile and Emigration with a gradient of 10 per cent, which is linked to the museum's entrance level by a ramp. The seven by seven grove of 6 metre (20 foot) high concrete columns is also at a 10 per cent tilt and is planted on top with Russian olive (*Eleagnus*) shrubs. To the east of this is the Walter Benjamin Playground with a water channel well and sand area. The Paradise Garden and Robinia Garden are beyond. At the Robinia Garden a spiral ground sculpture is set within the existing false acacia (*Robinia pseudoacacia*) trees while next to it is the cultivated Paradise Garden: the metaphor is that of the untamed power of Nature represented by the *Robinia* trees.

To the north and cleaving though the museum is a narrow space that the landscape architects Cornelia Müller and Jan Wehberg liken to a Berlin *hof* or courtyard – the Paul Celan Court, named for the poet and Holocaust survivor. This may be so, but the courtyard, which functions as a service route to the museum, is not an ordinary *hof*: it has a paving pattern based on drawings by Celan's wife, Gisèle Celan Lestrange, and is surrounded by the large masses of Libeskind's walls. These paving patterns extend south under the museum building towards the Holocaust Tower and there between the Tower and the Hoffmann Garden is a sole tree (*Pawlonia tomentosa*) – Paul Celan's favourite. Back along the north part of the building is the Hollmannstrasse, an old street which was retained but cut across and planted.

As well as having a meaning of their own the gardens feature as part of an east-west green belt within the wider green planning of the city. It is a place of green trees over the sombre gravels, a place where life springs from remembrance.

Top right: The concrete columns of the ETA Hoffmann Garden in the foreground with Libeskind's zinc-clad museum behind and the detached concrete Holocaust Tower to the left. Immediately behind that is the red tiled roof of the Prussian Collegienhaus.

Right: Detail of setts laid in a grass surround.

Opposite: The ETA Hoffmann Garden and surrounding areas change dramatically with the seasons.

Above: In the Paul Celan Court the zinc building façade and the courtyard paving become one composition.

Right: Paul Celan Court: detail with seat.

Far right: The paving pattern in the Paul Celan Court is based on the drawing of Celan's French wife, the artist Gisèle Celan Lestrange.

Left and top: The Paradise
Garden with its spiral
fountain which becomes a
water course.

Above: Plan.
1 Hollmannstrasse, a
memory of old Berlin
2 Paul Celan Court
3 E T A Hoffmann Garden of
Exile and Emigration

4 Roses
5 Walter Benjamin
Playground
6 Paradise Garden
7 Robinia Garden

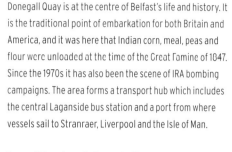

Donegall Quay
Belfast, Northern Ireland, UK, 1995-2001
Camlin Lonsdale

Donegall Quay is at the centre of Belfast's life and history. It is the traditional point of embarkation for both Britain and America, and it was here that Indian corn, meal, peas and flour were unloaded at the time of the Great Famine of 1847. Since the 1970s it has also been the scene of IRA bombing campaigns. The area forms a transport hub which includes the central Laganside bus station and a port from where vessels sail to Stranraer, Liverpool and the Isle of Man.

Donegall Quay is part of a much wider programme in recent years to regenerate and develop the whole of Belfast's riverfront. The quayside scheme is an extension of a much larger project to the south along Laganbank by landscape architects Robert Camlin and Paul Shirley Smith of Camlin Lonsdale.

The quayside is located between the Lagan and Queen Elizabeth bridges and faces the River Lagan weir, a new half tide barrier erected to raise the water level upstream, to which a footbridge was added in 1996. Essentially, the quayside project is an exercise in rescuing a city space that had been torn apart since the 1940s - first by Luftwaffe bombing, then by highway engineers and finally by terrorist activity. The once tight-knit composition of streets, quays, squares and dignified buildings had been broken up. New building, particularly the large Royal Mail sorting office, had also disturbed the urbane and civilized scale of the old quayside. One original feature that did survive is the Custom House (1854-7) designed by Charles Lanyon. The architects have used this as a centrepiece for a composition of two lines of poplar (*Populus* sp.) trees, which lead from the Custom House to the new Lookout, a pier projecting into the River Lagan upon which sit the steel cube and tower of the Millennium Beacon. Materials used include the simple paving of grey metamorphic schist from Switzerland, a

Berlau timber ramped deck, toughened glass side panels with stainless-steel rails and iroko wood hand rails. This is an exercise in close detailing. On the quayside close to The Lookout is *The Fish*, a 10 metre (33 foot) long sculpture by John Kindness of a salmon, which represents the return of fish to the newly cleansed River Lagan. *The Fish* is covered with ceramic tiles, which represent aspects of Belfast's history.

The development's other organizing feature is the Albert Memorial at the west end of Queen's Square, which runs inland alongside the Custom House. The memorial is the focus of a secondary axis which leads to the Lagan Weir and which is composed of a curved segment of horse chestnut trees (*Aesculus hippocastanum*). The weir forms the base of a cross-river footbridge which descends by a curved ramp to Donegall Quay and which is lit up in blue at night.

This modest and appropriate design forms part of Robert Camlin's professional contribution to his home city. It follows his work on Laganbank, which lies to the south. The Liverpool Bar by the quay, once the haunt of terrorists, is now listed in tourist guidebooks as one of the places to see in Belfast. As Robert Camlin has said, the aim was 'To invest the city centre with the quality of public realm it deserves.'

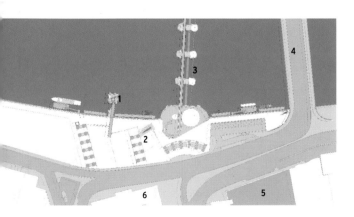

Above: Plan.
1. The Lookout
2. *The Fish*
3. Lagan Weir
4. Queen Elizabeth Bridge
5. Queen's Square
6. Custom House

Top: The nineteenth-century Custom House and the Millennium Beacon (to the right) seen from the Weir Bridge.

Opposite: The Millennium Beacon with its accompanying galvanized steel 'cube' (constructed by shipbuilders Harland & Wolff) on The Lookout. Beyond are the Lagan Bridge and the Weir footbridge.

Far left: *The Fish* by John Kindness is clad in ceramic tiles and contains a time capsule.

Left: The Lookout and Millennium Beacon seen from the Quay with its crushed granite resin-bonded paving in the foreground. In the distance are the great yellow cranes of the Harland & Wolff shipyard (where the Titanic was built), which dominate the city centre.

Above: On The Lookout, facing the quay and *The Fish*. Wooden benches are arranged around the Millennium Beacon (top right).

Left: Toughened glass
panels provide safety
without impairing views of
the quay and the water.

Above left: Detailing of the
junction between the ramp
leading from the quay to
The Lookout.

Above right: The Millennium
Beacon 'cube' of steel with
the anchor mast shrouding it off
in the background.

Invalidenpark
Berlin, Germany, 1992-97
Christophe Girot

North of the River Spree and east of the Berlin-Spandauer Ship Canal is the Oranienburger Vorstadt, a district which lay outside Berlin until the nineteenth century. In 1843, before the area had been built up, 6 hectares (15 acres) were made into a park designed by Peter Joseph Lenné, the great Prussian landscape gardener. In 1854 a column, the Invalidensäule, was built there to commemorate the Prussian soldiers who had died suppressing the 1848 Revolution. Towards the end of the nineteenth century Lenné's park was reduced by half in order to provide ground for the new Charité Hospital to the north and the Gnadenkirche (1895) to the south. The area had many associations with the Prussian army and the Emperor, but nearly all of it was to be destroyed. The church was bombed

in the Second World War and the remains of the park became a parking area for the East German Volkspolizei. The surviving walls of the ruined church were demolished in 1967.

Upon German reunification Federal Ministries moved into Invaliden Strasse and the area has gone from being on the periphery of East Berlin to becoming a central government and administrative area. With this renewal came the idea of re-establishing the remaining space as a new 2.7 hectare (6½ acre) park and in 1992 a design competition was held, which was won by the French landscape architect Christophe Girot. Though he was director of the Ecole Supérieure de Paysagisme in Versailles in the 1990s and keeps his practice there, Girot is not a typical Versailles-educated *paysagiste*. He began his education at the Environmental Planning Faculty at the University of California, which led him to Berkeley where he eventually taught. Now he is professor at ETH Zurich, the Swiss Federal Institute of Technology. With this international background Girot straddles the French, Anglo-Saxon and Germanic traditions of landscape design education.

Girot's goal at Invalidenpark was to refer to place and history, but in a controlled manner. He comments on the design thus:

On looking back I realize that this project was only able to come about at a time when the memory of the Wall was still fresh in everyone's minds. Like all memories, it will disappear. I didn't want to recreate the Wall, but rather underscore a certain moment in Berlin's history.

The park is in three parts. To the south, alongside Invaliden Strasse, narrow 50mm (2 inch) joints of granite paving are filled with grass. As it moves north the paving rises and the

grassed joints become wider until eventually grass supercedes granite. Across this paved and semi-paved area is laid a great rectangular basin orientated north-south across the paving alignment. There are also lines of gingko trees (*Gingko biloba*) crossing the parallel lines of paving. In the basin sits a tall, sloping water wall down which water cascades into the pool rather like a children's slide. The granite-faced wall slopes down to the grass towards the north where ruins of the Gnadenkirche foundations have been revealed. The centre of the park is planted with a grove of trees and a lawn while along the northernmost edge trees are planted in rows like a regiment on parade. There is also a playground with blue rubber safety paving for children living in nearby housing.

Embracing the two southerly portions of the park is a rectangular frame of gravel path, which rises 600mm (24 inches) above the lawn to the north, but along Lindenstrasse sinks 600mm (24 inches) below street level. The park is a series of levels – only the water in the basin is horizontal. For the centre Girot had originally proposed woodland with flowery glades, but instead the solution reached with the City has been for a more subdued effect with oak trees (*Quercus* sp.), rhododendron and ivy (*Hedera* sp.).

True to the architect's aims, this is a design that accepts history and commemorates the site, but in a very simple way. At the opening Girot quipped: 'Is this a park or a plaza, either way it is no carpark?' ('Man weiß nicht genau, ob hier ein Park oder ein Platz ist, auf jeden Fall kein Parkplatz.') This is the story of a capital city, once divided, which is finding itself again.

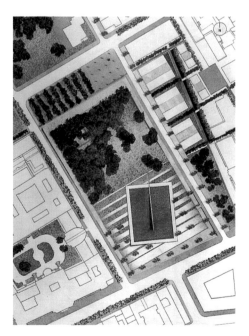

Above: Site plan. The sloping water wall and pool are at the bottom, where the effect of grass graduating into concrete can clearly be seen.

Top right: Looking south to the water basin with its wide rounded granite edge, with the bands of granite and grass to the left.

Above: Simplicity is
achieved with oak trees,
grass, and gravel paths. The
park is a more controlled
version of Bernard Huet's
comparatively overdesigned
Parc de Bercy in Paris,
where similarly existing
trees lie in the middle
of paths.

Right: A distant view of the
sloping water wall seen from
the wooded area in the
middle of the park, looking
south towards Invaliden
Strasse.

Top: Looking across the basin northwards.

Above: At night the park is transformed by strategic lighting. The hulk of the water wall seems to disappear while the water itself is illuminated.

Top: By day the sloping
granite water wall
dominates – locals call it the
Sprungschanze (ski jump).

Above: Detail of the channel
running along the water wall
with the shallow basin behind.

MeSci
Aomi, Koto-ku, Tokyo, Japan, 2001
George Hargreaves Associates

MeSci is the handy title of the new Tokyo National Museum of Emerging Science and Innovation, an interpretation centre and research institution devoted to new science and technology. Located on Aomi, one of the newly reclaimed islands in the western part of Tokyo Bay, MeSci forms part of the Tokyo Academic Park – indeed the whole area is extremely new. The island was only reclaimed in 1995 and the go-ahead for the Academic Park was given in 1998. The area is a sort of university city occupying 6.6 hectares (16 acres) of west-facing waterfront space. MeSci was opened in 2001 with total development costs of ¥100 billion.

The Academic Park is organized in rectangular plots, like a business park, and MeSci shares its rectangle with IAST (the National Institute of Advanced Science and Technology). The block to the south is occupied by the Tokyo International Exchange Centre with student housing and facilities for international students. The MeSci building was designed by Nikken Sekkei and rises eight storeys to form a fairly chunky, rather postmodern block with hints of Bakelite wireless styling. This is contrasted by eight storeys of elegantly curved curtain wall glazing on the entrance frontage.

The MeSci site area covers 2 hectares (5 acres) which Hargreaves has organized in parallel lines projecting at right angles away from the building. The gardens are a series of spaces, each with a scientific theme. On the southern, main entrance side of the building is the curtain wall of glass and an urban plaza where formal pyramid landforms emerge from an informal lake. The sculptural forms express the colliding and fusing of molecules. The hackberry tree (*Celtis sinensis var. japonica*) contrasts with the controlled ground form. The western gardens relate to the main galleries – the undulating landforms and wave walls represent the light, sound and electronic waves studied in science. In the central promenade rolling landforms with randomly placed wind sculptures remind visitors of the winds in the bay. This promenade continues and links all ten institutions in the Tokyo Academic Park.

Since he began practising in 1985 George Hargreaves has been known for his work on reclamation sites, often on waterfronts, and for campus masterplanning, which has extended to projects such as the 2000 Sydney Olympics. Often his work has involved recycling sites, for example Byxbee Park (1995) in San Francisco or the recent Waterfront Park in Louisville, Kentucky. At MeSci he has brought a sense of history and place to a newly reclaimed site. Certainly it is creative, but it is also functional: planting and features are appropriate to an exposed seafront site. But what is particular about this scheme is that it has created a concentrated sense of locality.

Above: The main entrance and lake with characteristic Hargreaves landforms.

Top right: The building seen from the west with the research wing on the right and the main galleries in the centre. Beyond is the adjacent National Institute of Advanced Science and Technology. From the building parallel wavy walls extend outwards and provide shelter to people and plants – this is an extremely exposed and windy seaside site.

Above and right: Once inside, the gardens at MeSci become intimate sheltered spaces which are full of interest. Stone is used extensively, and in this case the wave patterns recall the work of Alain Provost at Parc Diderot in Paris. Beyond the garden is the viaduct of the Yurikamome rapid transit rail link to downtown Tokyo.

At night the gardens are transformed by the effects of the lighting, which rakes across the stone forms.

Daylight creates very
different effects. In this
project Hargreaves has fully
exploited the Japanese
facility for working with stone.

Insel Hombroich
Neuss, Germany, 1985–
Bernhard Korte

Insel Hombroich constitutes one of the great acts of private landscape patronage of the late twentieth century. It is a *Gesamtkunstwerk* as interesting and challenging as Louisiana in Denmark, the Kröller-Müller Museum near Arnhem in the Netherlands, or Donald Judd's Chinati Foundation in Marfa, Texas. The museum was founded in 1985 by the Düsseldorf businessman and art collector Karl Heinrich Müller on a 26 hectare (64 acre) site by the River Erft, south-west of Neuss.

The project began as a place to house Müller's wide and growing art collection, which ranges from Khmer and Chinese buddhas, Rembrandt etchings and Cézanne watercolours to the works of Joseph Beuys. The collection is housed in eleven naturally lit galleries designed by the sculptor Erwin Heerich; now in his eighties, Heerich was a contemporary of Joseph Beuys at the Düsseldorf Academy

after the Second World War. The Düsseldorf architect Hermann H. Müller gave technical assistance. The galleries are simple geometrical structures with walls of reclaimed brick. On the inside the white spaces are as sophisticated as any city centre art gallery. These are introverted spaces; occasionally a leaf lies on the floor as evidence that this is an environment that stands outside the urban world. One significant feature of the museum is that the art is unlabelled: you see it for what it is, and judge it for what you see. There are also no security guards. This is indeed an extraordinary place.

Situated not far from the Ruhr Basin industrial area and set within a modern agricultural landscape crossed by motorways, the approach to the museum passes the remains of old NATO bases. Within this mundane setting is an oasis, a place separate from the daily world, which is described as the Island, or *Insel*. Müller originally acquired an actual small wooded island on the River Erft, on which there was a nineteenth-century garden. To this was added some arable land, subsequently restored to wetland by Bernhard Korte. There are pollarded willows, pools and wild flower water meadows, and now the area has grown to the heights of the terraces at the edge of the flood plain. More recently a separate extension has been added, which is not open to the public, on the site of a former NATO rocket base; this comprises a music conservatory, a number of artists' studios and the International Institute for Biophysics. This area is more forbidding and spartan, surrounded as it is by defensive berms and threaded through by military roads.

Also on the site is a permaculture farm, and the museum entrance fee includes a meal at which visitors can enjoy apples, bread, garlic, jam and other fruits of the land. There are two artists in permanent residence: Anatol Herzfeld (who was a pupil of Beuys) and Gotthard Graubner, who works in his own studio near the entrance building and advises Müller on the collection. Thus the whole collection is an act of patronage enriched by the contribution of the artists involved. Other artists stay for short periods at the former rocket base.

Elements of park, wetland, wood, river and garden come together in this site. But the overall effect is of something managed by a natural, not man-made, process: even the old, formal box-hedged garden is carefully tended to give a somewhat abandoned appearance. It may be contrived, but the contrivance is very relaxed: the garden elements seem about to be overwhelmed. This is an ecologically and romantically managed landscape, best viewed in the late autumn, or in late winter with frost on the trees. In the summer it appears very green, perhaps less elegiac and over-busy. Rather like the great landscape gardens of the eighteenth and nineteenth centuries, this is a place where landscape design acts, in Sir Geoffrey Jellicoe's words, as 'Mother of the Arts'.

Above: The former agricultural fields are now a land of long grasses and reeds, particularly when flooded in winter, and a rich habitat for wildlife and birds.

Right: Streams thread their way through this remade landscape. Coppiced willows provide evidence that this is a very intelligently managed environment.

Top right: Entering the Insel Hombroich down these steps is like finding a lost world – an area of former agricultural fields remade into wetlands and woods as they might have been, a sort of ecological ideal.

Opposite: A line of birch trees (*Betulus* sp.) lines one side of the old nineteenth-century garden. At the end of the walk is the circular Graubner Pavilion designed by Erwin Heerich, who always sites his buildings so that trees do not have to be felled.

Above: A shady pool in the nineteenth-century garden is typical of the riverside land along the Erft.

Right: The wetland areas consist of grassland which floods in winter, and pools edged by woodland and marked by coppiced willows.

Above: The island garden in September: the box hedges have grown clumpy, and the herbaceous plants look wild and overgrown.

In the distance is the Graubner Pavilion. Some of the planting on the island dates from 1820, when the Rosa House was built, but this garden dates from the beginning of the twentieth century.

Right: A view from the riverside to the edge of the flood plain terrace with the gallery beyond.

Opposite: Lines of close-planted poplars enclose the Lonq Gallery. Some of Herzfeld's Cor-ten steel figures can be seen in the foreground.

Above: From art gallery to wood in just one step: the view from the Long Gallery.

Above right: A timber bridge designed by Erwin Heerich leads to the Lonq Gallery.

Right: The Tadeusz Pavilion, housing Norbert Tadeusz's larqe paintinqs, is set into the bluff of the river terrace overlooking the valley.

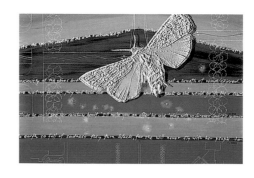

Northam Mulark Aboriginal Community Settlement Project
Northam, Western Australia, 2000
Grant Revell and Rod Garlett/University of Western Australia and Northam Mulark Aboriginal Community

This is a story of a people finding their home (their *karluk*), and also one of reclaiming their place in a society, their right to exist. In the words of Rod Garlett, Mulark Aboriginal leader:

In January 1933...Our people who had made their homes on the reserve were rounded up like sheep and sent to Moore River Native Settlement along with many other families. The excuse given was that the people were spreading disease, this eventually was proven to be untrue... Let us develop this reserve as a place for our people to come, a place where they can feel the presence of our loved ones who in their life time knew this place as home. (From *Northam Aboriginal Reserve 8383 Local History* typescript)

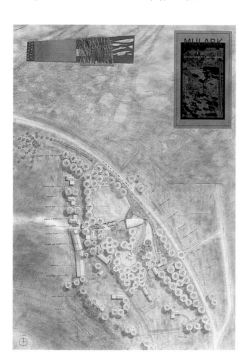

The Northam Mulark Aboriginal Community are part of the wider Noongar Aboriginal people who continue to live throughout south-western Australia. In 1946 the members of the Mulark Aboriginal Community were allowed to return from the Moore River Settlement, and in 1984 the Northam reserve was vested in the Aboriginal Lands Trust.

The Survey Map of the area allocates plot A8313 - 2.2936 hectares (5½ acres) - for the 'Use and Benefit of Aboriginal Inhabitants'. It is an unenclosed fragment of a landscape otherwise subdivided by the surveyor's line. Northam is nearly 100 kilometres (60 miles) north-east of Perth and is now an area predominantly of wheat and sheep farming. Europeans first came to Northam in the 1830s and it now has a population of 10,500. The town is expanding and plot A8313 is surrounded by suburban and semi-rural development.

The fight for their own space is part of the wider Noongar battle for a just settlement with the *whitefellas*, the European immigrants, who have denied them their landscape; removed, forcibly marched and resettled them; 'concentrated' the Aboriginal population; imposed curfews and taken children away from parents and relatives. Space means not just land, but also social and cultural space - and of course the idea of individual and exclusive land 'ownership' is not part of traditional Aboriginal culture

This is also the story of a project by landscape architecture students from the University of Western Australia. Since 1997 these students have been involved with Indigenous communities. In March 2000 twelve University of Western Australia Landscape Architecture students and twelve Murdoch University Environmental Science students worked on the Northam reserve project.

The 2000 study was just part of the process of recognizing the value of the Noongar Aboriginal way of life and attempting to atone for past wrongs. On a practical level the students studied proposals for a historical museum, a community hall, an arts stage, play areas, *Mia-Mias* (temporary-stay huts) for the extended Aboriginal families, *Kumpa Mia-Mia* (toilets) and shower facilities and parking. But on another level students learned about the invasion of Australia, understanding race relations, and participating in a dialogue with the Noongars. Indeed while working with the Mulark Aboriginal Community the students encountered disapproval from some *whitefellas* in Northam for working with the Indigenous inhabitants of Western Australia.

The students explored design themes reflecting Aboriginal culture, and of course in this dialogue the Community had the final say. The important places were not just the birthing site or the waterhole, but also the original foundations, floors and pathways left by their exiled forefathers in the 1930s. The design studio became a continuing affirmation of the Mulark Aboriginal Community and a learning process for landscape students. The project also led to the competition entry for Reconciliation Place, Canberra, in 2001 by a joint team of *blackfellas* and *whitefellas*. This is just part of the long and continuing story of cultural identity in Australia.

Above: Landscape architecture student Francis Kotai's overall plan for the Northam Aboriginal Community is also an artwork in its own right.

Top right: The work at Northam led to the competition entry for Reconciliation Place, Canberra, which used the story of the Bogong Moth. The background painting is by Jody Broun, acclaimed Aboriginal artist and member of the design team.

Opposite: Plan showing the arrangement of vegetation on the site.

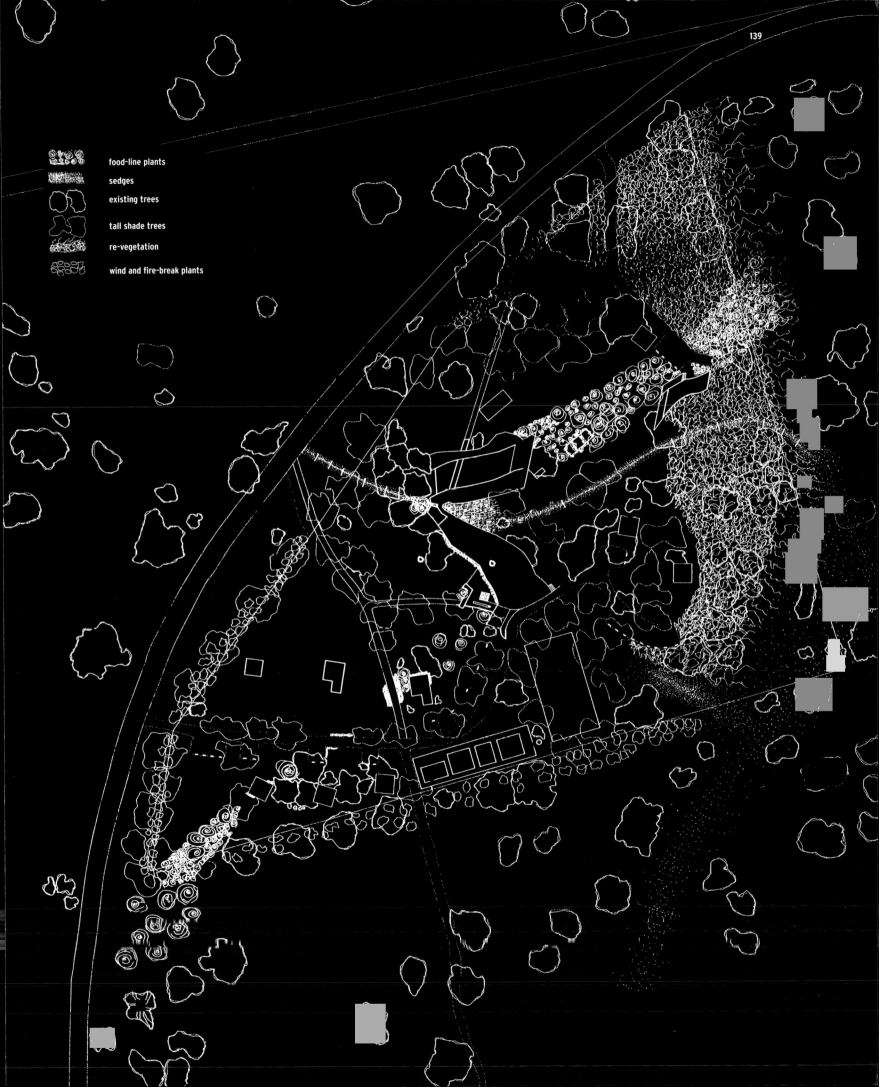

food-line plants

sedges

existing trees

tall shade trees

re-vegetation

wind and fire-break plants

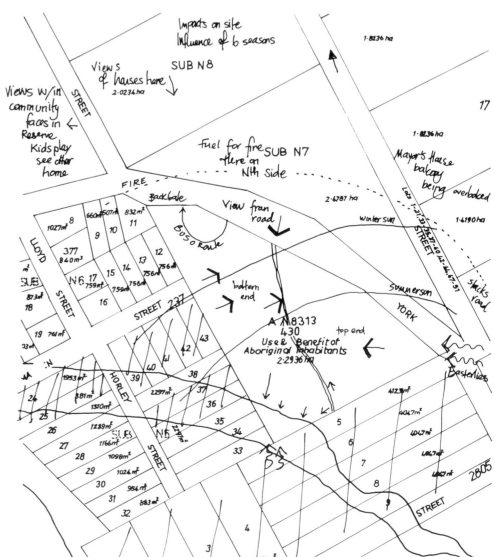

Top: Tracing evidence of the community as it was before and after the forcible resettlement of 1933.

Right: In this map landscape architecture student Lisa Archer, a project member, documented her community meeting notes over the existing survey map which allocates the Northam Aboriginal Reserve property.

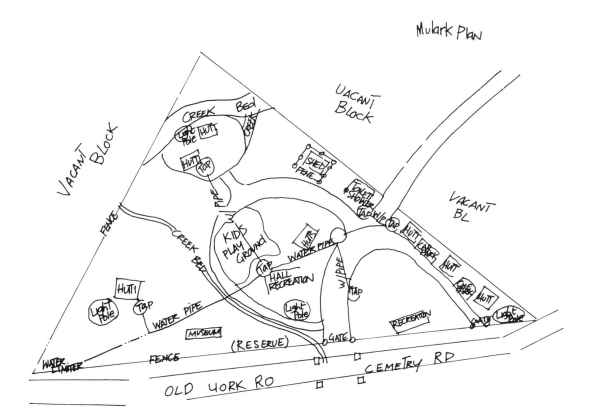

Mulark Plan

Left and above left: Excavations revealed traces of the pre- and post-1933 community structures, including the foundations of hut floors and surrounding brick pathways.

Above right: Members of the Mulark Aboriginal Community with University students and staff during the project.

Top: Map drawn by members of the Mulark Aboriginal Community. The map shows the placement of buildings, open areas and playgrounds and takes into account areas of family and historical significance.

The Garden of Australian Dreams
Canberra, Australia, 1997-2001
Room 4.1.3

Australia is a new country, still defining its own identity. As part of that process - and to celebrate the upcoming centenary of Australian political federation in 2001 - the Federal government held a competition in 1997 for the design of an Australian National Museum in the capital, Canberra. The winning team were the firm of architects Ashton Raggat McDougall with Robert Peck von Hartel Trethowen. The new building houses both the National Museum of Australia (NMA) and the Australian Institute of Aboriginal and Torres Strait Islander Studies (AIATSIS). The 10 hectare (25 acre) site is on the Acton Peninsula on Lake Burley Griffin at the heart of Canberra and its position has created a new waterfront for the city.

The accompanying Garden of Australian Dreams had an ambitious competition brief of its own: to represent a country's and a continent's mythology. Indeed it forms part of a wider landscape scheme for the Museum and for the Acton Peninsula involving the new Uluru Axis - a line linking the Federal Parliament House with the centre of the continent's landmass, its navel, the *Uluru* (formerly known as Ayer's Rock).

The garden is laid out as an internal courtyard within the semicircular sweep of the museum buildings and faces away from the lake (though there is a glimpse of it through the buildings). Visitors approach the garden via a promontory on the open western side. On the south side is the Aboriginal Gallery of Australia, a zig-zag form which cuts into the elliptical form of the buildings. The northern edge of the garden is bordered by water and is largely a hard landscape except for a small grass plot known as The Backyard. This is one landscape design that seems to dominate the surrounding buildings.

The garden's main design feature is its concrete surface, painted to represent maps of Australia, on which visitors can walk and read complex layers of cultural information. Parts of the concrete were painted dry or had oxide colours brushed into the wet surface while elsewhere oxides were washed in to give a mottled effect. The surface was then stabilized against ultraviolet rays with a layer of sealant and will have to be resealed every five years.

Two main maps were used to form the ground surface: one a standard English language map and the other David Horton's 1990s map illustrating the linguistic boundaries of indigenous Australia. These maps show two histories of Australia. The main maps are interwoven with vegetation, soil and geology maps, road maps and maps of electoral boundaries. Overlaid across all of this is the Mercator Grid and the Australian Map Grid. Other graphic references include the 5,309 kilometre (3,297 mile) long Dingo fence - the world's longest continuous structure. A bright yellow line through the garden indicates the Western Australian state border.

The Garden is laden with text. The word 'home' is spelled out in the various languages spoken in Australia today. Elsewhere there is the signature of Edmund Barton, federated Australia's first prime minister.

In addition to the garden's two-dimensional mapped surface there are several three-dimensional elements: a *camera obscura*, a grotto and tunnel, a row of tilting, twisting Italian alders, a large dead eucalyptus fallen in water, a flood gauge, a grid of surveyor's poles, a bush garden and a suburban garden. And, laughing at all this, is the garden's very own gnome, a figure in the shape of an 'antipodean' (a monstrous mythical creature once thought by Europeans to inhabit the antipodes).

Richard Weller and Vladimir Sitta of Room 4.1.3 are two of the most intriguing and intellectually challenging landscape designers working today. Richard Weller sums up the project thus:

'The Garden of Australian Dreams is a microcosmic representation of Australian self-consciousness, based on virtuality and simulacra as opposed to mimesis of "nature". It is also a project which claims to be a landscape design about landscape design, explicitly challenging landscape expressions.'

Right: The black box *camera obscura* sits in the centre of the garden, while the red wedge marks the Uluru Axis.

Top right: The Uluru Axis - a line connecting Canberra to the heart of Australia - is expressed as a wide red strip running through the design.

Another view of the *camera obscura* with a raised grotto to the right. To the far right are a surveyor's pole and part of the Dingo fence. The broad, dark grey bands of concrete represent the Mercator world grid while the Australian Map Grid is shown by the thin blue lines.

Left: A cubist detail.

Above: The area known as the Living Room with the Backyard and pool beyond. On the far side of the cube there is a white projection screen for nighttime viewings.

Top: The sky composed.

Above: At night the garden and museum buildings are lit, changing the value and emphasis of the forms.

Above: The final stages of construction: the *camera obscura* is to the left and the dark grey lines of the Mercator grid cross the garden. In the foreground the languages of Australia can be seen while beyond are the British colonists' place names. On the far side the coastline and the Pacific Ocean are represented by water.

The eastern end of the tunnel, The landscape of lines, words and meanings is tangled and knotted 'as a metaphor of a nation's interwoven pluralist destiny'.

chapter 5 ecological diversity

Ecology is one of the most significant developments in twentieth-century science. Its study has led to applied ecology, which has been a major influence in landscape architecture, town planning and, to a lesser extent, architecture since the 1960s. In the 1950s teachers such as Brian Hackett at Newcastle in England first began to put forward ideas about ecological landscape architecture. These ideas were then more widely disseminated through the teachings, works and writings of Ian McHarg of Penn State University, particularly through his book *Design with Nature* (1969).

Much earlier in the century, from the 1920s, the writings of J.P. Thysse led to the establishment of *heemparks* and *heemtuinen* which represent the native landscape types of The Netherlands (peat garden, clay garden, sand garden and dune forest). In the 1960s the artist Louis Le Roy carried forward these ideas in his designs for gardens such as Herrenveen in The Netherlands (1970), which re-used the material of the site. Such ideas were also found in Germany where, for example in the 1980s Hermann Barges was recycling materials and planting in an ecological way in Berlin's Kreuzburg district.

In France Gilles Clément, co-designer of Parc Citroën-Cévennes (1993), is known as a *paysagiste*, novelist and writer. 'Le Jardin Planetaire' (1998), an exhibition celebrating the ecological world at the Parc de la Villette in Paris, is perhaps his best known work. Whether dealing with biodiversity, elements of recycling or the creation of habitat types, designers have faced the challenge of realizing these ideas in different ways.

Herbert Dreiseitl has concentrated particularly on one element: water. Atelier Dreiseitl's Potsdamer Platz redevelopment design (pages 150-153) uses surface water that has run off roofs and pavements and recycles it, effectively creating a more sustainable and pleasant place, a place where you can dip your feet in the water in the middle of summer.

Three of the British projects illustrated in this chapter were funded by the National Lottery and relate to ecological demonstration, education and understanding. The Eden Project in Cornwall (pages 154-157) is partly educational, and partly recreational. The former kaolin quarry has been re-used to create tropical, Mediterranean and temperate gardens to Land Use Consultants' designs. At the Welsh National Botanic Garden at Llanarthne in South Wales Kathryn Gustafson has also designed interior gardens, but in a slightly more conventional way, which sit under Foster's glass dome (pages 158-161). Here design is about creating different habitat types within a sculptural setting. In Yorkshire, on the site of old colliery workings, Andrew Grant has designed a natural educational resource devoted to Planet Earth (pages 162-165). This is an example of using ecological habitats and recycling systems as the forefront of a project. The Jubilee Centre campus at the University of Nottingham (pages 166-171) is also devoted to education and research and so themes similar to those at the Earth Centre - surface water recycling, creation of wetland habitats - are used as the backdrop to a scheme which is about creating a healthy environment on what was a brownfield redevelopment.

In Spain the Barcelona Botanic Garden (pages 172-175) shows a very different approach to its British counterparts: administratively it appears much more traditional, while as a design it is more strongly geometric with its use of triangles loosely draped across a hillside.

The chapter's two final schemes are on the West Coast of the United States. The Solar Living Centre in northern California (pages 176-181) is devoted to solar power and water management and is a demonstration of how a wasteland can be turned onto a place of ecological and scenic value within ten years. In Portland, Oregon, a defective stormwater drain presented an opportunity for Murase Associates to create a stormwater garden (pages 182-185) formed by a water detention basin. The project is now a publicly accessible demonstration of the stormwater and run-off management policies of the Portland Bureau of Environmental Services.

Potsdamer Platz Redevelopment

Berlin, Germany, 1998

Atelier Dreiseitl

The newly redeveloped areas around Potsdamer Platz lie right at the centre of reunified Berlin. The fact that much of this centre has water running through it is largely due to the work of one man, Herbert Dreiseitl. His watery creation threads through the public spaces of the new centre, forming still pools, stippled waves and rhythmic patterns as it falls over water structures and weirs. It also fulfils a number of functions: it acts as a 'buffer' to protect against flooding, reduces pollutants into the nearby canal, and acts as a temperature modifier – as well as providing a source of urban delight.

The water runs from Potsdamer Strasse to Marlene-Dietrich-Platz via a channel, the Nordgewässer. At Marlene-Dietrich-Platz the water opens into a large trapezoid-shaped basin, Haupgtewässer, which in turn leads to the Landwehrkanal. In total there is now a water body of 1 hectare (2.5 acres), containing 12,000 cubic metres (35 cubic feet) of water, with a shoreline of 1.6 kilometres (1 mile).

Before World War II, Potsdamer Platz had been Berlin's hub: the city's equivalent of Piccadilly Circus or Times Square. During the war the area was heavily bombed, however, and in later years the Berlin Wall ran right through its centre, from north to south, rendering it a wasteland. Following German reunification, the redevelopment of this part of Potsdamer Platz was commissioned by a consortium which included corporations such as Sony and Daimler-Benz. The masterplan, covering 7.5 hectares (18.5 acres), was designed to link the city's historic cultural area with the new commercial centre of Potsdamer Platz and Leipziger Platz.

Dreiseitl first worked on the area in 1991 as part of Richard Rogers's controversial and unsuccessful masterplan team, and had also worked on Ökostadt – the wider Berlin city ecological planning study. In 1992 he was reappointed as part of the new team, led by Renzo Piano and Christoph Kohlbecker. Piano's successful proposals saw moving water as a metaphor for the healing process between East and West: it represents a gap that has now been bridged. Piano also sees water as confirming Berlin's close relationship with nature, connecting the green of the Tiergarten to the north to the water of the Landwehrkanal to the south.

As part of the water management system there are five underground cisterns, which act as settling tanks. They have a total volume of 2,600 cubic metres (92,000 cubic feet), of which 900 cubic metres (32,000 cubic feet) is left available for heavy rain. In addition the pools can accept a

150mm (60 in) rise, which provides an extra 1,300 cubic metres (46,000 cubic feet) of buffer. On leaving the cisterns the water passes through planted purification areas: phosphates are removed by the water passing through the root zone of reed beds. *Phragmites communis* is the dominant reed, but Dreiseitl also uses *Juncus inflexus* and *Juncus effusus* as well as *Iris Pseudoacoris* and sedges such as *Carex gracilis* and *Carex acutiformis*.

Long-term computer simulation shows that the application of Dreiseitl's water management regime in the new building development at Potsdamer Platz will not increase surface water runoff and discharge for the city. And 70 per cent of the water comes from the roofs, half of which are green roof gardens as is usual practice in Berlin in order to slow water runoff and maximize biomass.

Water and integrated water management has been a recurring theme in Herbert Dreiseitl's career. 'Water is a very mystic and a very deep element that has to do directly with life', says the designer. 'If we don't learn to understand water differently, to work and behave with water differently, we'll have no healthy water anymore, and ... no world to give our children.'

Left: Cooling toes in the still waters of the Hauptgewässer: it is the variety of water effects that makes Dreiseitl's scheme at the Potsdamer Platz redevelopment so special. Dreiseitl modelled the water movement using both computer-aided and life-size models.

Top right: Free access to water is a fundamental principle of this design – which means the water has to be both clean and inviting. Here, shallow weirs create water patterns.

Opposite: The Hauptgewässer pool outside the Musik Theater in Marlene-Dietrich-Platz. Visitors can walk around the edge of the water, or pass over it via a bridge. Note how cars are not completely excluded, but are slowed by tight turnings; pedestrians have absolute priority here.

Eden Project

Bodelva, Cornwall, UK, 1994-2001

Land Use Consultants

Described as a 'global garden for the twenty-first century and beyond', the Eden Project is the brainchild of record-producer-turned-gardens-producer Tim Smit. Smit had earlier been the driving force behind the restoration of the Lost Gardens of Heligan, also in Cornwall. The other main protagonists at Eden were horticulturists Philip McMillan and Peter Thoday, who had also worked at Heligan.

In 1994 Tim Smit conceived the idea of building the world's largest greenhouse in a former china clay quarry near St Austell. Smit recalls, 'Slowly but surely it developed into an understanding that it would not be enough to just have plants, it had to represent a new way of thinking about living.' This led to the concept of showing wild and cultivated plants in a range of exotic climate houses, as well as establishing an outdoor temperate garden. Total funds raised came to £86 million ($128 million), which came from the National Lottery and the European Union as well as from banks.

The south-facing site extends over 15 hectares (34 acres), and the quarry is 60 metres (200 feet) deep. Landscape architects Land Use Consultants (LUC), led by Dominic Cole, acknowledged the history of Cornish china clay extraction: the overall design is based around the curved slopes and haulage routes of the old quarry. Cole says that he 'did not wish to impose a design, so we built a design up.'

Approaching the site you soon catch glimpses of the Earth Centre's domes, or Biomes, which at first sight look like giant soapsuds mounting the quarry walls. Architect Nick Grimshaw's brief was to provide two greenhouses: one a humid tropical area, the other a warm temperate zone. (The idea of a third, desert house was omitted from the first phase but is still planned.) The two Biomes are vast geodesic domes formed of hexagons plus the occasional pentagon, and clad with three layers of ETFE (ethyltetrafluoroethylene).

Inside the larger, tropical house are displays designed by LUC of plants and crops from the Amazon, West Africa, Malaysia and Oceania, with waterfalls, streams, pools and stage-set displays of Malay houses. The Warm Temperate Biome deals with Mediterranean climate-zone vegetation from California, South Africa, Western Australia and the Mediterranean basin itself. Linking the two glazed Biomes is a 500-seat restaurant with a walkway above and a grass roof. Outside the Biomes, the clay pit itself features a 12 hectare (30 acre) outdoor landscape of cool temperate plant displays. These range from Chilean temperate rainforest through Cornish heath and Atlantic oakwood to crops such as wheat, sunflower and lavender.

The Cornish landscape generally comprises a Celtic small field pattern enclosed by high banks, and this theme of introspective enclosure continues in the design of the Eden Project's approach infrastructure. LUC have successfully disposed the 1,000 parking places in terraces around the pit, using traditional stone-faced field banks in clever ways to contain and disperse the impact of the parking. This screening largely continues until one is inside the Visitor Centre, which is located on the edge of the quarry pit.

The construction and landscaping of the Eden Project was beset with enormous technical problems. The China clay material is loose and unstable, and rather than using sprayed concrete, meshes and gabions the slopes are stabilized with vegetation supplemented by geotextiles such as coconut matting. The water table is above the floor level of the pit, and water is collected via swales and then pumped out or used in irrigation. The original site contained no topsoil and so soil manufacture was vital. Local mine waste was used, together with sand and reject clay from local companies. Forestry bark was used as the organic component for interior soils, and composted, domestic green waste outside.

The quarry is now a fertile, vegetated landscape of slopes and ramps, with a lakeside arena for events at the bottom. The pit has been compartmentalized into interlocking 'sabre' shapes, defined by ramped paths. The structural tree planting follows the curves, but the sabre shapes have been cut across and down the slope by patterns of straight lines formed when one type of planting gives way to another. Tim Smit calls this 'Picasso meets the Aztecs'.

The star of the show is the huge Humid Tropics Biome, which after just one season had become a jungle. The Warm Temperate Biome is smaller, its vegetation more contained, less fast growing, and of greyer green hues. This is both a demonstration of concern about ecological diversity and a great popular success, with more than 1.5 million visitors in 2001.

Right: A view into the 60 metre (200 foot) deep quarry, with the Visitor Centre to the right. The two Biomes rise up on the far side of the quarry: the Humid Tropics dome to the left and the Warm Temperate dome to the right. Linking the two is a grass-roofed restaurant building, with lake and arena in front.

Opposite: The site in September 2001, still raw-looking during its first season of growth.

Above: Crops in the foreground, with the Warm Temperate Biome beyond. Single species crops were one of the most successful features of the outdoor landscape in the first year of opening, and include sunflowers, tea and hemp.

Right: The Eden Project viewed from the serving edge above, showing how established vegetation soon takes effect.

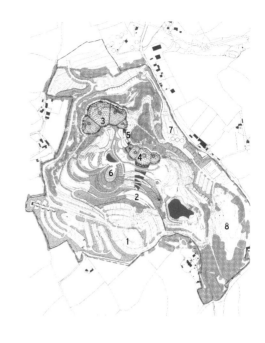

Top left: Swales are vital to ensure good drainage on these steep slopes.

Above: Celtic bank walls in the 'Wild Cornwall' display.

Right: Geotextiles were used for steep slope establishment to prevent erosion. This picture was taken in September 2001.

Top right: Masterplan of the site. The main access road is at the top left of the plan.

1. Parking
2. Visitor Centre
3. Humid Tropics Biome
4. Warm Temperate Biome
5. Restaurants
6. Arena
7. Service area
8. Future expansion

Top: The Prairie Area, leading to the Humid Tropics Biome.

Above left: The Humid Tropics Biome is an interior landscape that becomes a tropical world. Inside the massive geodesic dome are recreations of jungle habitats from the Amazon, West Africa, Malaysia and Oceania.

Above right: Olive trees and stone terraces in the Warm Temperate Biome. This dome includes displays of vegetation from California, South Africa, Western Australia and the Mediterranean.

Great Glasshouse, National Botanic Garden of Wales

Llanarthne, Carmarthen, Wales, UK, 1997-2000
Gustafson Porter

The National Botanic Garden of Wales is a major new botanic garden of international significance. The National Lottery funded the £43 million ($60 million) project, and the landscape costs were £1.3 million. The garden is set in the 230 hectares (568 acres) of Middelton Hall, a late eighteenth-century parkland established by William Paxton. Dyfed County Council began the restoration of the parkland and gardens of which the new botanic gardens will occupy 66 hectares (162 acres). The Great Glasshouse stands near the site of the old house – designed by S.P. Cockerall and destroyed by fire in 1931 – on a low but commanding hill. The glasshouse is sunk low into the ground, its concrete substructure covered with turf, so that only Foster and Partners's great roof is visible from the grounds.

The dome consists of a 95 metre (309 foot) long, 55 metre (180 foot) wide single-glazed steel arch roof, which covers an interior landscape for the garden's Mediterranean displays. The roof glazing feeds rainwater into tanks beneath the building for reuse in irrigation and flushing lavatories. To optimize energy usage, the building's internal environment is computer-controlled. This system – designed by mechanical engineer Max Fordham – adjusts the supply of heat by opening and closing glazing panels in the roof to achieve desired levels of temperature, humidity and air movement. A biomass furnace maintains the Great Glasshouse at 5°C (40°F) above ambient temperature and keeps it from falling below 9°C (48°F). One-hundred and forty-seven computer-controlled vents regulate the natural airflow, while high-level fans blast air to simulate the windy Mediterranean climate.

The collections, supervised by curator Wolfgang Bopp, comprise Mediterranean climate zone plants from California, the Mediterranean basin, the central coastal region of Chile, the Cape region of South Africa, and Australia.

Kathryn Gustafson has recreated a sculpted rock ravine landscape, which cuts 5 metres (16 feet) into the ground in planted terraces of a warm, light sandstone. Stone textures vary from sawn-faced to split and fissured. The ground around the edge rises 1 metre (3 feet) and so gives a total drop of 6 metres (20 feet). The brief required high cliff walls and shady valleys; seasonally bare areas which then would grow and flower with annuals; dry and wet areas; water conditions ranging from stagnant to flowing; and dry stream beds which would sometimes flood.

Gustafson's intention was:
'to create a dropped-in landscape, working from the horizon line [so that] you raise the visible horizon within the glasshouse to such an extent that the roof of the building disappears into the sky, appearing less a cover than as something up there.'

The collections include olive groves (*Olea europaea*), Acacia forest and spring annuals. The planting arrangements are based on the effects of form, density and colour and not just on plant type or geographical region. The plants are still organized by region, but also by aesthetic composition, for example plants of yellow-green, silver-green and dark green foliage are grouped according to colour. Both the lowest points in the ravine and the highest plant density correspond with the highest portion of the roof.

The ground is mulched with crushed light sandstone gravel. The gravel size becomes finer nearer the entrances and coarser within the landscape. There is a ramp on a gentle 1:20 gradient on the south side, which creates a curve linking the entrance to the pool and water areas. Stone steps allow an ascent to the building concourse. Along the south side of the ramp is a steel-caged, gabion retaining wall filled with the same sandstone rocks, the size of which reduces higher up the wall.

The idea is to allow free access – the only restraints are protection rails along the edges of ravines, and even these are set back from the edge by 1 metre (3 feet) to reduce their visual impact. Elsewhere planting location and density and the size of the stone define areas of accessibility. The elements in metal and wood – the bridges, rails and steps – are to be seen as non-natural elements brought into the 'natural' landscape, which Gustafson has designed. The aim is to create a coherent landscape so that the display is much more than just an interesting plant collection under a big roof.

Left: The collections seen from the entrance.

Top right: The narrow gorge with the roof above.

Opposite: Water splashes down a vertical ravine into a pool below.

Above: The sandstone rock ravines and terraces accommodate different habitats of wet and dry. The floodable gorge can be seen below while olive trees (*Olea europaea*) are planted above at ground level.

Right: Gustafson's early model of the ravine.

Opposite: Large olives (*Olea europaea*), *Echium* sp. and oleander (*Nerium oleander*) are planted in the sandstone gravel mulch. Note the opening vents in the roof above, which allow the temperature to be controlled.

Earth Centre

Conisbrough, Yorkshire, UK, 1996–

Grant Associates

The Earth Centre has remade 170 hectares (420 acres) of old coalpits and limestone workings into an ecological education centre-cum-theme park that celebrates planet Earth. The first phase opened in April 1999. The Earth Centre deals with the basic elements of earth, fire, water and animal, vegetable and human life. Environmentalist John Letts devised the concept and this was carried through by Jonathan Smales, a former director of Greenpeace UK. Landscape architects Derek Lovejoy Partnership and engineers Battle McCarthy produced the masterplan in January 1997. Work began on site in autumn 1997 with a land reclamation project run by Ove Arup and Partners, which continued until spring 1998.

The site is set in the valley of the canalized River Don and the ground material comprises colliery waste. Two hills have been created from colliery spoil and a subsidiary of the Don has been revegetated to create a park-like setting of meadows and woodlands through which Sustrans, the national cycle network, now runs.

Landscape architect Andrew Grant worked for Battle McCarthy on the masterplan and took over in 1997. The idea was to make use of the land, provide employment and bring the site 'back from the dead'. He retained the few industrial artefacts that remained, the naturally revegetated limestone rock terraces on the hillside and the grooves of old railway sidings. The valley setting has a strong history of prehistoric, medieval and industrial settlement and the designers wanted to remember the history, not only by keeping what little remained, but by setting up views to historic features outside the Earth Centre and by telling the story of mining and quarrying.

Visitors enter across a refurbished industrial bridge over the River Don which leads to a spiral of white limestone and black coal spoil. This leads to Solar Point, a triangular plaza paved with riven York stone from nearby Wakefield. On one side lies the limestone faced Planet Earth Gallery by Feilden Clegg and the gabion-walled Conference Centre by Bill Dunster. On the other side, Feilden Clegg have also designed the Eat building, which is clad in green oak and where visitors can eat a range of organic foods. The plaza has a photovoltaic roof. The triangle is set on an axis which lines up with Conisbrough Castle to the south-east and towards a proposed 'Ark' building by Future Systems to the north-west.

The 20 hectares (50 acres) of Phase One are fan-shaped in plan set along the straight canalized portion of the River Don. The entrance plaza line forms another side. The third side of this fan consists of wide curves, which repeat as a series of terrace gardens. A curved path within the River Don side repeats a reverse curve to create a giant eye shape. To the north and east, on reclaimed land, is the sweeping parkland.

Running diagonally across Phase One is a straight axial route from the river to Alsop and Störmer's tropically planted and transparent Water Works building. The route continues to the large Water Tank and then to the Whaleback, a reshaped colliery spoil heap. Cadeby stream has been retained and forms a tree-lined valley. Set between the main lines of Grant's design are theme gardens: wetlands along the river, a play area, reed and willow coppices and an orchard.

The gardens and buildings play a part in telling the story: restaurant visitors wash their hands and are reminded that the waste water goes to the Water Works, where bananas and other plants feed on the soap and nutrients and clean the water. The water is then treated in the gardens and is used for irrigation or for flushing toilets. Similarly the energy flows within the Earth Centre are explained and monitored - visitors are invited to contribute by generating bicycle-powered electricity. Future phases include more facilities for school parties, including residential accommodation and the Ark building.

This landscape is very consistently designed by one hand. Comparisons with British Garden Festivals of the 1980s have been made: the Earth Centre is similarly compartmentalized, has a number of themes and is set on reclaimed land. But Andrew Grant is adamant that 'this is not a Garden Festival' and indeed it is more serious and interesting in its ambition. Like the Eden Project, the Earth Centre began with the help of British National Lottery funding. Having begun as a 'big bang' project it is now changing to a more incremental type of development such as that of the Centre for Alternative Technology, Machynlleth (see pages 8 and 10) in order to realize its original long-term ambition.

Right: Split panorama of the picnic space in front of the Water Works. The steel framed concrete basement building houses biological waste water treatment and is part of the sustainable sewage and water management system. The Whale, a mound created from colliery pit heaps, can be seen on the skyline.

Top right: At the entrance to the Earth Centre lies Solar Point. Its 1000 square metre (10,700 square foot) space frame is covered in photovoltaic cells. The Planet Earth Gallery is on the right, and the Eat building on the left.

ABOVE: Reeds growing in the freshwater pool next to the Earth Centre's 'Natureworks'. Ten years before this picture was taken this was a derelict colliery wasteland: now it is an educational resource for school parties and children from all over the country.

Right: Little remains of the old colliery structures apart from this reinforced concrete bridge spanning the River Don. It now forms the entrance bridge to the Earth Centre.

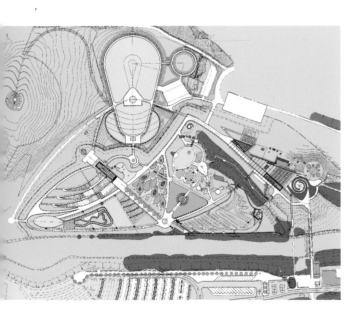

Above: Plan of phases one and two showing the River Don to the south and the curved paths around the theme gardens and the pools. These lead to the site of the proposed Ark building (Phase Two) designed by Future Systems (top/north of plan).

Top left: The Conference Centre, by Bill Dunster Architects, is walled with rock-filled gabions and lies next to Solar Point.

Top right: View from the entrance café terrace over the River Don and to the surrounding limestone hills beyond.

Centre left and right: The freshwater pool is surrounded by woven willow fences with basketweave peepholes at different heights.

Above: The 'Waterworks' display explains the processes that take place in the pool outside, helping children – and adults – learn about freshwater ecology.

Above: This scheme is about exhibitions and teaching areas set within a new landscape. Outside are newly created pools and reed and willow vegetation, while inside the 'Natureworks' building by Letts Wheeler is an exhibition gallery for water and terrestrial ecology.

Right: Aerial view showing the River Don, taken in 1999 while grass was being established. To the bottom are the parking areas and railway station. The two bridges lead to the triangular Solar Point with its black and white spiral and from here curved paths embrace the theme gardens and wildlife areas.

University of Nottingham Jubilee Campus
Nottingham, UK, 1999
Battle McCarthy

Built on the former Raleigh bicycle works just west of Nottingham city centre, this £22 million ($33 million) development forms the School of Computer Science and Information Technology, School of Education and Business School, as well as student halls of residence and accommodates 1,000 students and staff. At the centre is a library and computer facility, in a reversed conical building that projects into the lake. Previous incarnations of the site tell a potted history of Nottingham's industrial past: they include coal mining, railway sidings, the old Nottingham Canal (culverted in 1954), a waste destruction facility, a tractor depot and a timber yard.

The 7.5 hectare (18 1/2 acre) site is arranged in three 'belts', with the inner belt comprising a series of lakes. The buildings and parking areas to the north are bent to form a 'boomerang' shape embracing the belt of lakes. Beyond the lakes is a belt of woodland, with some areas of older trees. The 'boomerang' faces south-west to catch the afternoon sun, while *brises-soleil* break the sun's glare. Grass mounds together with the woodland belt provide pleasant views while screening the new development from suburban Nottingham beyond. Visual relief is vital for computer users.

The planning scheme is a response to the UK government's policy of encouraging 'brownfield' development. The designers have laid particular emphasis on allowing wildlife to flourish while also dealing with the fundamental problems of building on contaminated former industrial land. The campus is situated in the corridor of the River Leen. Geologically it comprises predominantly river gravels and sand, with a 2 metre (6 1/2 foot) layer of made land on top. Industrial use had resulted in a very high pH, occasional excessive salinity, high boron levels and high concentrations of copper, zinc and nickel, which can be toxic to plants and animals. In the built-up area of the campus, the land was either 'capped' under buildings or covered with imported topsoil; the contaminants that are left remain immobile due to the high pH. In case rainwater should ever lower the pH sufficiently to mobilize the metals, the tree pits are isolated from the surrounding substrate. Row tree planting consists of a line of horse chestnuts (*Aesculus hippocastanum*) planted along a spine road (alongside which runs the main drainage channel, or swale), and similar row tree planting in the parking areas.

The lakes provide a new wetland habitat in the river corridor, and act as a buffer between buildings and people and wildlife. Dug to a maximum depth of 1.2 metres (4 feet), they are lined with bentonite clay so as to both retain water and exclude contaminants. Bentonite expands and contracts, allowing root penetration without leaks. Excavated material was used to cover the bentonite layer; this was both clean and of low fertility in order to avoid excess nutrients in the lakes. The lakes are fed by surface water runoff from roofs and car parks, which is treated to remove hydrocarbons. The water leaves the lakes via an outfall. Oxygenating plants are being grown in the lakes, and water is recirculated using mechanical pumps. Air diffusers will maintain oxygenation until a balanced ecosystem is established.

The landscape design follows the principles of sustainable development and this includes balance between cut and fill; the reuse of all site materials; the use of low-cost, super efficient, mechanically assisted heat exchangers for ventilation; and designing the buildings to maximize thermal mass. Green roofs vegetated with stonecrop (*Sedum*) help reduce the flow of rain runoff. The aim was to find a solution that would combine functional form with low energy use and economical maintenance in a holistic approach to campus design.

Right: View of the Main Lake from the library, showing the earth mounds and woodland belt beyond.

Top right: Clad in Western Red Cedar, the lakeside halls of residence were designed by Michael Hopkins. The Learning Resource Centre and Library is to the right.

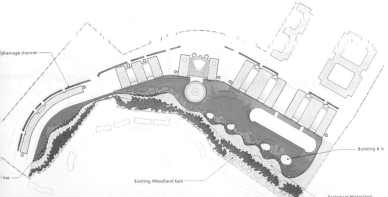

Left: Plan of the south-west facing site, showing the band of woodland (yellow and brown), the lakes and then the buildings fronting the lakes. The broken blue line represents the swale, or main drainage channel, whereby gravity feeds water through wide-diameter pipes to the lakes.

Above: A gabion-lined channel connects the Small Lake to the Mill Pond. On the far side is the Business School and circular Library.

Overleaf: The lakes allow a close juxtaposition of the urban with woodland and meadow. Small islands in the lake allow ground-nesting birds some safety from rodents and urban foxes.

drainage channel

Bunding & H

Existing Woodland belt

Ecological Hinterland

Above: Small islands line the
Main Lake and in the picture
these merge with the
mounds behind. Along
the mounds are bands
of wetland and marginal
plants, then water-meadow
grasses, and finally a mix of
dry meadow grasses on the
top of the earth mounds.

Above and left: Although this is a large urban university campus, used by hundreds of students, a range of planting has been possible. These include a natural habitat of reeds, irises and meadow planting (above), and a turfed 'people island' (left), which acts almost as a common area or village square for the students.

Above: The botanic gardens overlook Barcelona from the slopes of Montjuic. This panorama reveals how the triangles 'fray' to allow a close fit to the land form.

Grassed plots await the future growth of what promises to be a key Mediterranean botanic collection.

Right: Site plan: the entrance, shop, ticket booths and parking are at the bottom of the drawing.

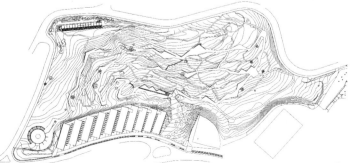

Right: Steep slopes are easily eroded in heavy rainfall, hence the importance of path-side drainage channels, which direct water into storage tanks for recycling as irrigation water.

Solar Living Center
Hopland, California, USA, 1996
Land and Place

Real Goods began by selling solar panels, but has grown to provide everything for the environmentally conscious ranging from yurts to whisky barrels (sold as garden water tubs). Founder John Shaeffer conceived the Real Goods Solar Living Center, established in 1992 in Hopland, California, as a venue for educational workshops. Since 1998 the Solar Living Institute has been a separate, not-for-profit organization. The aim behind the project was to create a sustainable landscape around a museum dedicated to solar energy. 'For years it was just too expensive to mine the sun: the technology was too expensive. But all that's changed now,' says Shaeffer.

The landscape architects are Stephanie Kotin and Christopher Tebbut, who together form the design build firm Land and Place. They both studied horticulture at the Round Valley Garden and the Royal Botanic Gardens at Kew, England and have an extensive knowledge of plants. Kotin categorizes the context of the site as elements which informed the design: the meander of the floodplain, the associated flora, local agriculture and its grid and rhythm, and the wilderness of the surrounding hills, clad in coastal oak forest.

Hopland is north of Santa Rosa in the Sanel Valley, some 150 kilometres (95 miles) north of San Francisco and 80 kilometres (50 miles) inland. The 5 hectare (12 acre) site is wedged between Highway 101 and a railroad track next to the Feliz Creek - it had previously been used as a highways dump site. The site was a dry exposed wasteland with only one tree, a valley oak (Quercus lobata), and its transformation into a fertile landscape is representative of this enterprise: idealistic commerce. The project takes solar energy as its theme, but uses aquifer-delivered water as its counterpoint. The Solar Living Center is situated over an aquifer. A photovoltaic direct pump system raises water into a 13,600 litre (3,000 gallon) re-used redwood tank, which overflows into a series of flowforms, and then, via a rill, into fountains and pools. The water is then recirculated by another solar pump. On the way to the pump the water is used for irrigation, evaporation cooling, education and fun features. Temperatures in the area can rise to 43°C (110°F) in the summer. As the sun grows hotter, and the need for water is greatest, the pumps work harder.

The landscape design follows a spiral, which is centred on the museum building by architect Sim van der Ryn. The building is located at the spiral's centre, just above the level of the floodable area. In contrast with the sinuous spiral geometry the site is bisected by the traditional agricultural grid, but orientated north-south rather than east-west, and with formal avenues of trees to mark the cardinal directions. Similarly, the points of solstice and equinox sunrises and sunsets are marked by stones. The site also needed to be screened from Highway 101, a source of noise,

dust and pollution. A curving earth berm was constructed that faces and screens off the highway. Rising out of the berm, facing the highway, is the Memorial Car Grove where trees grow through ironically re-used gas-guzzling Buicks from the 1960s.

Within these organizing systems are spaces that have become places. Immediately south of the Center building is a courtyard with a living tree arbor trained to form a canopy over a fountain, an area where many of the Center's activities take place. To the north is a series of pastoral landscapes set around a lake with pools, gardens, orchards and a small representation of valley oak (Quercus lobata) forest. In some ways this arrangement resembles a Dutch heempark - a place with a series of representative and local landscape types.

Not surprisingly, the Center also boasts productive horticulture areas including orchards of nut trees and a kitchen garden with espaliered pears, apples, soft fruit and annual vegetable beds, double-dug in the French manner. Wilfredo Tinico of Land and Place stayed on after the building and site development to lead the management of the landscape. No pesticides are used and entrance is free - this is a serious place for learning about alternative technology and ecological landscapes.

Left: The view from the Center Building with Mount Duncan beyond. The Tree Sculpture Fountain comprises eight gray poplar trees (Populus canescens macrophylla) which are being trained to grow into a dense canopy. Each tree represents a cardinal direction.

Above and opposite top:
Water descends from the
recycled redwood tank and
is aerated by the flowform
sculptures set within a
planting of California
fuchsia (*Fuchsia* sp.)
and monkeyflower
(*Mimulus* sp.).

Right: Plan showing the
water system in relation to
the land. Water flows from
the tank (on the right),
passes through the Center
with its 'living sculpture
fountain' then into both the
Upper Pool (centre) and the
Lower Pool which has a
floating solar fountain. The
water then feeds a native
wetland restoration area,

beyond which is a riparian
restoration area along the
Feliz Creek (left).

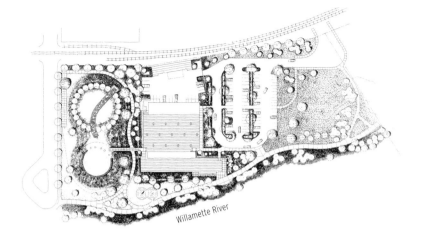

Willamette River

Opposite: The curved flume through which stormwater passes into the detention basin is filled with crushed basalt stone and surrounded by reeds which assist sedimentation and biofiltration. Periodically it is necessary to dig out solids which deposit in this flume.

Top: Plan showing the detention basin to the left, the laboratory building in the middle and the parking and expansion areas to the right. The riverside walk passes along the whole site and connects with Cathedral Park.

Above: The detention basin shown half full. Holes on the side of the flume feed water into the basin which has a permanent water area. Portland can have dry summers, however, and in July and August the pond tends to become anaerobic and smelly.

project credits

Mas de los Voltes

Landscape	Fernando Caruncho
Construction company	Contrucciones Figueras
Nursery	Viveros Planas
Irrigation and pumping	Grimpola, SA

Market Place & Water Steps

Landscape & water design	Atelier Dreiseitl
Architect	Büro Walter
Stonework	Family Hettingel
Client	Hattersheim City

Sony Complex

Landscape architect	Peter Walker William Johnson and Partners
Architect	Murphy/Jahn, Inc., Architects
Engineer	Ove Arup & Partners
Client	Sony Corporation

Kitigata Apartments

Landscape architect	Martha Schwartz, Inc.
Design team/ Project contributors	Paula Meijerink, Michael Blier, Shauna Gillies-Smith, Chris MacFarlane, Kaki Martin, Don Sharp, Lital Fabian

Agnes Katz Platz

Architect	Office of Dan Kiley: Dan Kiley, Peter Morrow Meyer, Terence Lee, Nanda Patel
Artist	Louise Bourgeois
Construction management	Oxford Development Co.
Contractor	Massaro Inc.
Fountain consultant	Dan Euser Waterarchitecture
Client	The Pittsburgh Cultural Trust

Campus Green

Design team	George Hargreaves, Mary Margaret Jones, Glenn Allen, Steve Hanson, Christian Werthman, Tom Ryan, Jim Grimes, Kendra Taylor, Chris Reed, Betsy Boykin, Ken Haines
Architect	Champlin-Haupt
Local landscape architect	Martin Koepke
Engineers	KZF Design
Fountain consultant	Dan Euser Waterarchitecture

Ibaraki Prefecture Government Offices

Architect	Shodo Suzuki
Consultant	Matuda-Hirata, Architect & Associate
Contractor	Dainihon Doboku Company

NTT Headquarters

Landscape	Diana Balmori, Principal, Balmori Associates, Inc., with Masahiro Soma, Principal, Soma Landscape Planning Co, Ltd.
Architect	Cesar Pelli & Associates, Inc.

Ørestad

Landscape architect	Jeppe Aagaard Andersen
Client	Ørestadsselskabset A/S
Design team	ARKKI A/S - Architects and Town-planner/Jeppe Aagaard Andersen
Landscape Architects Engineer	Rambøll A/S

Tramvia Park

Landscape architect	Enric Batlle Durany & Joan Roig Duran (Batlle i Roig)
Collaborators	Iván Sánchez Fabra, student of architecture/Teresa Galí Izard, technical agricultural engineer
Client	Mancomunitat de Municipis del Area Metropolitana de Barcelona Ministerio de Fomento

Borneo Sporenburg

Credits	Adriaan Geuze, Wim Kloosterboer, Yushi Uehara, Sebastiaan Riquois
Client	New Deal

Rådhusplads

Consultants	KHR/AS architects/subconsultant: Anders Nyvig A/S (traffic conditions); KKRI (Consulting City Engineers, Copenhagen); The City Engineer Office; Road Adm./subconsultant: Hifab Bygherreombud A/S (construction management and supervision) The City Architect Office
Contractors	General contractor for terminal building and public lavatories: Pihl & Son A/S City hall square including bus stops, utilities & paving: The Municipality of Copenhagen paving: Petri & Haugsted stone stairs: Londero Mosaik concrete casting of slabs at bus stops: Creteprint
Client	Copenhagen Municipality, 4th Dept./Copenhagen Transport Authorities (HT)

Nasu History Museum

Architect Kengo Kuma & Associates
Cooperative architect Ando Architecture Design Office
Structural engineer K. Nakata & Associates
Mechanical engineer P.T.Morimura & Associates
General contractor KAWADA Industries, INC.

Parc de la Théols

Landscape architect Desvigne et Dalnoky
Contractor Moser Val-de-Loire
Client Ville d'Issoudun

Whiteinch Cross

Landscape architect Gross Max
Artist Adam Barker-Mill
Project manager Rock DCM
Contractor Land Engineering
Client Glasgow 1999/ Whiteinch and
Scotstoun Housing Association

Enschede Station

Landscape architect OKRA landschapsarchitecten
Architects Martin Knuijt and Christ-Jan
van Rooij in co-operation with
I/AA Enschede, Sign Design,
Binnenbuiten and VanderTak
Architecten
Client City of Enschede

Matchworks

Landscape architect Brodie McAllister
Architect shedkm
Landscape contractor Adana Construction
Paving Marshalls
Tree grilles Broxap
Road studs Roadcraft
Gabions Tinsley Wire
Lighting Iguzzini

Volklingen Ironworks

Landscape architect Latz+Partner
Client European Centre for Art and
Industrial Culture UNESCO World
Cultural Heritage Völklingen Works

Ferropolis

Landscape Architect Büro Kiefer,
Landschaftsarchitektur Berlin
Architects Büro für urbane Projekte Leipzig
(Iris Reuther, Björn Teichmann),
Ian Ritchie, Andreas Hoffmann,
Inger-Johanne Tollhaas
Lighting designer Jonathan Park
Engineer Consultinggesellschaft für Umwelt
und Infrastruktur mbH, Halle
Client EXPO 2000 Sachsen-Anhalt Gmbh

Hedeland Arena

credits not available

Dionyssos Quarries

Landscape sculptor Nella Golanda
Architect Aspassia Kouzoupi
Client The Company Dionyssos Marble
S.E.

Negev Phosphate Works

Landscape architect Shlomo Aronson
Design team Eitan Eden and Yair Avigdor
Client Negev Phosphate Works
Geologist's Client Yair Levy

Südgelände Nature Park

Designers ÖkoCon and planland/Planungs-
gruppe Landscape Development:
Prof. Dr. Ingo Kowarik, Dr. Andreas
Langer, Ludger Schumacher,
Helmuth Knoll
Teamworkers Emma Phillips, Stella Junker-
Mielke
Client Grün Berlin Park und Garten GmbH

El Cedazo Park

Architects and Mario Schjetnan and
Landscape architects José Luis Pérez
Collaborators Marco Arturo González and
Martín Andrade
Client Aguascalientes State Government

Jewish Museum

Landscape Architects Cornelia Müller and Jan Wehberg
(MKW)
Architect Studio Daniel Libeskind
Engineers GSE Tragwerksplaner, Berlin & IGW
Ingenieurgruppe Wiese, Berlin
M&E engineer KST, Klima-Systemtechnik, Berlin
Lighting design Lichtplanung Dinnebier KG,
Wuppertal
Architecture construction Arge Beusterien und Lubic,
supervisor Berlin
Landscape contractor Günther Schumann GmbH, Garten-
und Landschaftsbau, Berlin
Client Land Berlin, Senatsverwaltung
für Bauen, Wohnen und Verkehr

Donegall Quay

Landscape Architect/ Camlin Lonsdale
Project Manager/
Contract Administrator
Engineer Kirk McClure Morton
Main Contractor F P McCann Ltd.
Steelwork Subcontractor J K Fabrications Ltd.
Artist John Kindness
Client Laganside Corporation

Invalidenpark

Competition and Phusis, Paris
design development
Project leader Christophe Girot
Design team Jean Marc L'Anton, Anja Mörsch,
Dominique Hernandez,
Alain Goldstimmer
Perspective drawings Frank Neau
Construction management Christophe Girot at Onne
Versailles in collaboration with
Manfred Fromme at Pala, Berlin
(landscape engineers)

MeSci

George Hargreaves (Design
Director) in collaboration with
Nikken Sekkei Ltd. (Architect
& Structural Engineer)
Project manager Tim Anderson
M&E engineer Kume Sekkei
Lighting design consultant Lighting Planners Associates
Sign consultant Hiromura Design Office
Sculpture Aijiro Wakita
Client Japan Science and Technology
Corporation

Insel Hombroich

Landscape design Dr Bernhard Korte
Architectural design Erwin Heerich
Technical architect Hermann H. Müller
Gardeners Brothers Köhler
Palaontobotanist Dr Knörzer
Assistance with planting Schöneck Schwegler
of perennial garden
Client Karl Heinrich Müller

**Northam Mulark Aboriginal
Community Project**

Grant Revell and Rod
Garlett/University of Western
Australia and Northam Mulark
Aboriginal Community

Garden of Australian Dreams

Project team Principals Vladimir Sitta,
Richard Weller
Team members Elizabeth Burt, Kioshi Furuno, Luca
Ginoulhiac, Scott Hawken, Silvia
Krizova, Pavol Moravcik, Maren
Parry, Daniel Firns, Karl Kullmann
Architect Ashton Raggatt McDougall
General contractor Acton Peninsula Alliance
Landscape contractor Urban Contractors Pty Ltd

**Potsdamer Platz
Redevelopment**

Water design Atelier Dreiseitl
Architects Renzo Piano; Christoph Kohlbeller
Main contractor Müller-Altwatter
Numerical simulations ETH-Zürich
Mechanical engineers Schmidt-Reuters Partners
Limnilogical consultants Technical University Berlin,
Prof. Dr. Ripl; Technical University
Berlin, Dipl. Ing. Schmidt;
Bodensee-Wasserversorgung,
E.Wendlandt; IGB Berlin,
Prof. Dr. Steinberg; University
Freiburg, Dr. Schröder
Clients Berlin City; Debis Immobilien

Eden Project

L.U.C. Design Team Dominic Cole, Lucas Greysmith,
Jane MacCuish
Architect Nicholas Grimshaw & Partners
Civil/structural engineers Antony Hunt Associates
Services engineers Ove Arup
Main contractor McAlpine Joint Venture
Ground preparation & E.H.Veerman
planting (external exhibits)
Paths, fencing, boulder wall Cormac
Tree surgery & hedging Simon Lackford
Waterfall Ritchie Mackenzie
Bamboo Rails Low Impact Design
Client Eden Project Ltd

**Great Glasshouse, National
Botanic Garden of Wales**

Internal landscape consultant Gustafson Porter (lead designer
Kathryn Gustafson)
Architect Foster and Partners
Structural engineer Anthony Hunt Associates
Services engineer Max Fordham and Partners
Project manager Schal International Management
Client National Botanic Garden of Wales

Earth Centre

Masterplanners/ Grant Associates
Landscape architects
Architects Feilden Clegg Architects/Alsop
and Störmer/Future Systems
Engineers Ove Arup & Partners
Infrastructure Atelier One Atelier 10
Irrigation Parker Associates
Grid shells Buro Happold
Soil scientist SGS
Landscape contractor Bernhard's Landscapes
Advanced tree stock Bellwoods Trees
Wildflower mixes Nigel Dunnett and James
Hitchmough

**University of Nottingham
Jubilee Campus**

Landscape architect Battle McCarthy (Mike Luszczak,
Brian Dunlop, Mike Brizell, Pippa
Henshall)
Ecologists Nicholas Pearson Associates/
Dr. Mike Wells
Architect Michael Hopkins and Partners
Engineer Ove Arup and Partners

Barcelona Botanic Garden

Design Team Carlos Ferrater, Architect/Bet
Figueras, Landscape architect/
José Luis Canosa, Architect
Collaborators Joan Pedrola, Botanist/
Dr. Montserrat, Botanist
Construction Carlos Ferrater, Executive
architect
Collaborators Bet Figueras/José Luis
Canosa/Urban Designs of City
Council
Builder Stachys, S.A.
Engineering Taller d'Engyniyeries S.A. Ignacion
Ortega
Client City Council of Barcelona

Solar Living Centre

Landscape Design/Build Land and Place
Architects Van der Ryn Architects, Ecological
Design Institute, Arkin Tilt
Architects
Sculptor Baile Oakes
Structural engineering Bruce King
Contractors TDM Construction, Land and Place

**Water Pollution Control
Laboratory**

Landscape architecture Murase Associates
Architecture Miller Hull Partnership
Architect of Record SERRA

index
Page numbers in *italic* refer to illustrations.

picture credits

The publisher would like to thank the following sources for their kind permission to reproduce images in this book.

7 top author
7 bottom photo Arie Koster from *De Groene Omgeving* (Schuyt & Co, Haarlem)
8 the author
9 the author
11 top the author
11 centre Gustafson Porter
11 bottom Bagnoli Project, City of Naples
14-15 Fernando Caruncho
16 top Laurence Toussaint
16 bottom Fernando Caruncho
17 Fernando Caruncho
18-21 © Atelier Dreseitl
22-23 Peter Walker
24 © Engelhardt/Sellin, Architekturfoto
25 Peter Walker
26-29 Martha Schwartz
30-31 © Arron Kiley
32-35 Hargreaves Associates
36-39 Shodo Suzuki
40-41 photos by Toru Waki/© Balmori Associates, Inc.
42 bottom left photos by Toru Waki/© Balmori Associates, Inc.
42-43 photo by Monma Kaneaki/© Balmori Associates, Inc.
44-45 Jeppe Aagaard Andersen
48-51 Eugeni Pons
52-53 top and bottom Geroen Musch
53 centre the author
54 top left and bottom right the author

54 bottom left Geroen Musch
55 Geroen Musch
56-59 Ole Meyer for KHR/AS
60-63 Kengo Kuma
64-67 Desvigne & Dalnoky
68-71 Gross Max
72-75 OKRA
76 bottom Nick Hufton/View
76 top-79 Brodie McAllister/ Chris Brink
82-83 © Latz + Partner
84-87 Büro Kiefer
88-91 the author
92-96 Aspassia Kouzoupi and Nella Golanda
97 Dimitris Kalapodas
98 top right Albatross
98 bottom Shlomo Aronson
99 Dubi Tal
100-101 Doron Horevitz
102-105 photos Andreas Langer/planland
108-113 Gabriel Figueroa Flores for GDU
114 top Bitter + Bredt
114 bottom © Luetzow 7
115 © Hélène Binet
116 centre © Hélène Binet
116 bottom left and right © Luetzow 7
117 top right Stefan Müller
117 bottom left © Luetzow 7
118-121 Camlin Lonsdale
122-125 Christophe Girot
126-129 Hargreaves Associates
130-137 the author
138-141 Grant Revell
142-147 Room 4.1.3
150-153 © Atelier Dreiseitl
154-157 the author
158 top right Gustafson Porter
158 bottom left © Michael Murray
159 Martine Hamilton Knight
160 top left © Michael Murray
160 bottom right Gustafson Porter
161 Martine Hamilton Knight
162 top right the author

162 bottom left and right Grant Associates
163 top the author
163 bottom Grant Associates
164 top left Grant Associates
164 top right the author
164 centre left Grant Associates
164 centre right the author
164 bottom right Grant Associates
165 top the author
165 bottom Grant Associates
166-170 Colin Philp
171 Battle McCarthy
172-175 Alejo Bagué
176 top right Lawrence Watson/Land and Place
176 bottom left © Richard Barnes
177 © Richard Barnes
178-179 © Richard Barnes
180 Lawrence Watson/Land and Place
181 Lawrence Watson/Land and Place
182-185 Scott Murase

author's acknowledgements

The author would like to thank Research Coordinator Susan Lawson, Commissioning Editor Philip Cooper and Project Editor Liz Faber from Laurence King Publishing, and also Mark Vernon-Jones for his design.

192